THE AMERICAN COCKTAIL

★

THE AMERICAN COCKTAIL ★

50 RECIPES THAT CELEBRATE THE CRAFT OF MIXING DRINKS FROM COAST TO COAST

BY THE EDITORS OF **imbibe** MAGAZINE

PHOTOGRAPHS BY SHERI GIBLIN

CHRONICLE BOOKS

SAN FRANCISCO

Library of Congress Cataloging-in-Publication Data available.
ISBN 978-0-8118-7799-2

Manufactured in China

Designed by **Anne Donnard**
Styling by **Christine Wolheim**
Photo assistant **Shay Harrington**
Typesetting by **DC Typography**
The photographer wishes to thank Karen Foley and *Imbibe* magazine for the
opportunity to work on such a fun and delicious project; road trip companions
and partners in crime Christine Wolheim and Shay Harrington for their creative
inspiration and support; and Brian Wagstaff and Mr. C for helping make the
shoot on location in Portland happen with ease. Happy imbibing, everyone!

10 9 8 7 6 5 4

Chronicle Books
680 Second Street
San Francisco, California 94107
www.chroniclebooks.com

★ ACKNOWLEDGMENTS ★

A.C.

Imbibe's mission is to celebrate the world in a glass. We highlight stories of the people, places, flavors, and cultures that make up the fascinating world of drinks, and it's hard to find more interesting inspiration than right here in America. A big thank-you to all of the incredibly talented bartenders who shared their recipes and expertise for this book, and here's to all of the endlessly creative distillers, brewers, roasters, winemakers, and farmers who help weave the unparalleled cocktail tapestry we enjoy across the country.

CONTENTS

A.C.

★ INTRODUCTION ★

AMERICA HAS A STORIED PAST WITH SPIRITS AND COCKTAILS. As immigrants from around the world settled in cities and towns across the country, they brought the culinary traditions that inform the way we drink today. Thanks to the industrious, whiskey-loving settlers of the South, we have Kentucky bourbon country, and if it hadn't been for nostalgic Italian immigrants, California's Bay Area might not have experienced its love affair with Italian amari.

While these influences remain as steadfast as ever, America's melting pot of culinary traditions has also spawned new trends across the country, from the fresh, seasonal cocktails of the West Coast to the classically inspired drinks of the South. What's more, uniquely American ingredients have found their way into some of the country's best cocktails, from bacon-infused bourbon blended with Carolina-made ginger ale to a loquat-and-lemon cocktail mixed with artisanal vodka made in Texas's oldest legal distillery.

Now you can experience these drinks for yourself. The fifty cocktail recipes presented here were gathered from talented bartenders across the country and feature regionally produced spirits, sodas, fruits, herbs, and even tea. Whether you're imbibing a Persimmon Margarita in Los Angeles or a Mint Julep in Louisville, the cocktails that define the American landscape are deliciously diverse. Consider this book your personal cross-country tour of America's most intriguing regional cocktail flavors, traditions, and stories.

Travel should always be this satisfying.

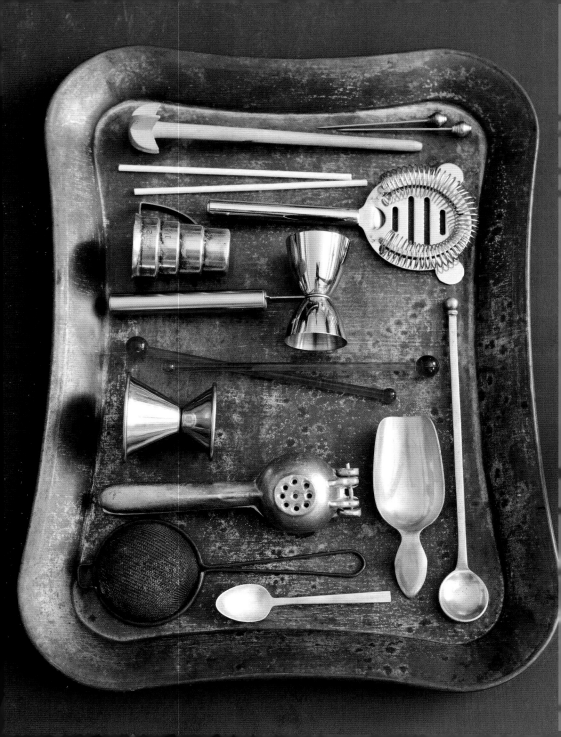

★ COCKTAIL BASICS ★

A.C.

In order to make great cocktails, you need to have a basic understanding of the tools and techniques required for home mixology. You don't need to purchase the most expensive tools, and you can find most of what we outline in this section very affordably either online or in your local grocery store or house-wares shop. *Imbibe* has reviewed most of these tools in previous issues and/or on our Web site, so you can also consult the magazine for recommendations (www.imbibemagazine.com).

TOOLS

Gearing up to mix cocktails requires a simple setup that you can add to over time as you get more serious about drink making. To begin, be sure you have a measuring glass, shaker, barspoon, muddler, Hawthorn strainer, fine-mesh strainer (which you probably already have in your kitchen), and some toothpicks. Over time, you can add items like a Boston shaker, a channel knife, specialty ice trays, an ice crusher, decorative cocktail picks, and other useful gadgets.

Barspoon: Usually about 12 inches long (but sometimes longer) with a swiveled shaft, barspoons are essential for stirring cocktails. You can also use them for measuring ingredients; 1 barspoon equals approximately 1 teaspoon.

Boston shaker: A two-piece cocktail shaker consisting of a glass mixing vessel designed to fit securely inside the top metal tumbler. The Boston shaker does not have a built-in strainer.

Channel knife: A small handheld tool designed to cut a fruit's rind when drawn over its surface, and perfect for creating citrus peels and twists.

Fine-mesh strainer: A small, handheld strainer with very tight mesh designed to keep particulates out of a finished drink. Often used for double straining cocktails. Also known as a tea strainer.

Hawthorn strainer: A stainless-steel strainer with a wire coil, which is designed to fit snugly over a mixing glass, enabling you to strain a cocktail into a glass. Often used in cojunction with a fine-mesh strainer for double straining cocktails.

Ice crusher: Available in both electric and hand-crank versions, these handy little machines are useful if you frequently need larger quantities of crushed ice.

Jigger: A tool used to measure liquid for cocktails. A jigger holds 1½ ounces.

Measuring glass: A small glass used for measuring out cocktail ingredients. Look for one with measurements in ounces.

Mixing glass: A pint glass or the bottom half of a Boston shaker—either glass or metal (often referred to as a "tin")—used for muddling ingredients, stirring drinks, or combining ingredients for shaken cocktails.

Muddler: A pestle-like tool used to crush fruit and/or herbs in a glass to extract their flavors.

Strainer: Refers to either the built-in strainer of a cocktail shaker or a stand-alone Hawthorn strainer.

Three-piece cocktail shaker: A metal shaker with a tight-fitting lid and a built-in strainer. Also known as a cobbler shaker.

Whipped cream siphon: A canister that uses chargeable gas cartridges to create and dispense whipped cream.

TECHNIQUES

Wondering what it means to dry shake? Not sure how to double strain a cocktail? Here's a nuts-and-bolts overview of some of the most common cocktail-making tricks and techniques.

Double straining: Straining a cocktail through both the strainer in the lid of the shaker (or Hawthorn strainer if using a Boston shaker) and a fine-mesh strainer held over the glass.

Dry shaking: Shaking a cocktail without ice.

Glass chilling: Chilling glasses that are used for cocktails served up (with no ice) to ensure a cocktail remains chilled once poured. You can do this by putting a glass in the freezer for a few minutes prior to using or by placing a few ice cubes in a glass and then discarding them before using the glass.

Glass warming: Rinsing a glass with hot water before using for a cocktail. Often used for hot cocktails to help the drink stay warm.

Layering: Separating a layer of cream or another liquid ingredient from the rest of the cocktail, such as in Irish Coffee. You can achieve this by slowly pouring the liquid over the back of a spoon on top of the drink.

Muddling: Using a muddler to press and/or break down ingredients, such as fruit and herbs, in the bottom of a shaker or glass.

Rimming a glass: Coating the edge of a glass with an ingredient of choice, most commonly sugar or salt, in such drinks as Margaritas and Sidecars.

Shaking: Using plenty of ice and shaking vigorously until the outside of the shaker is frosted—no wimpy shaking allowed. Cocktails that combine syrups, juices, or other ingredients that need to be well-incorporated with spirits are typically shaken.

Stirring: Using a barspoon and stirring with plenty of ice until the mixing glass begins to frost. Spirits-driven cocktails, such as a Manhattan, are generally stirred so as not to agitate the spirits too much by shaking.

GARNISHES

A garnish can be a cocktail's pièce de résistance. Whether it's a brandied cherry, a salted rim, or a playful citrus twist, garnishes often add just the right finishing touch to a cocktail, sometimes amplifying depth of flavor and/or aroma, and sometimes simply making a drink look more beautiful. There are many more types of garnishes not detailed here, but following are some of the ones most commonly used.

Cherry: Fresh cherries, brandied cherries, maraschino cherries, or Marasca cherries, such as those made by Luxardo and available at www.kegworks.com.

Citrus peel: A swath of citrus peel that is usually twisted over a drink to release the fruit's essential oils and sometimes placed in the cocktail as a garnish. To make a peel, use a vegetable peeler or paring knife. If using a knife, simply cut a thin piece of the peel, being careful not to include any flesh. The pieces can range from a round quarter size to a 1-by-2-inch piece.

Citrus twist: A thin piece of citrus peel that is usually twisted from both ends over the drink to release the fruit's essential oils before dropping it into the cocktail or resting it on the rim of the glass. To make a twist, run a channel knife across the surface of the fruit, getting as long of a piece as you desire (being careful not to get any fruit flesh), then coil the peel to form a twist.

Citrus wheel: A circular slice of citrus that is rested on the lip of the glass. To make a wheel, simply cut slices parallel to the tip of the fruit.

Fruit slice: A slice of fruit usually placed decoratively on the rim of a glass. It can run the gamut of options, from apples and peaches to kiwi or star fruit.

Rings: Decorative wheels of seeded peppers and chiles that can be skewered or dropped into a cocktail.

Skewers: Cherries, olives, and other ingredients that are placed on cocktail picks and rested across the rim of the glass or dropped into a cocktail.

Wedge: A lengthwise section cut from lemons, limes, or oranges.

GLASSWARE

Acquiring glassware is one of the most fun parts of having a home bar. As with your tools and ingredients, just be sure you cover the basics when you're starting out, then build your collection over time. And don't be afraid to mix and match—at *Imbibe*, we love mixing vintage glassware with new pieces. And if you want to use a coupe in place of a cocktail glass, go for it. One easy way to figure out what kind of glassware you need is to decide what top five cocktails you want to be able to make—then plan your glassware accordingly.

Cocktail: A V-shaped glass with a long stem, also known as a Martini glass, that is designed to serve "up" drinks and keep warm fingers away from the cold liquid.

Collins: A tall, 8- to 14-ounce glass that is often used for iced drinks and those with carbonated ingredients, as its slender design helps to hold the drink's fizz.

Cordial: A petite, 1- to 3-ounce glass used for aperitifs and digestifs, as well as very small cocktails.

Coupe: A stemmed, saucer-shaped, 4- to 8-ounce glass often used for classic cocktails and/or drinks that include sparkling wine.

Double rocks: Also known as a bucket glass or double Old Fashioned, this glass is common for such drinks as the Margarita.

Flute: A tall, stemmed, 6- to 10-ounce glass designed to keep Champagne bubbly and also used for sparkling wine cocktails.

Highball: Larger than a rocks glass but shorter than a Collins, this glass is most often used for drinks with cubed or cracked ice and carbonated ingredients.

Julep cup: Traditionally a short metal cup popularized by the Mint Julep.

Mug: A glass or ceramic cup often used for serving hot drinks, such as toddies.

Old Fashioned: Also known as a rocks glass, the 6- to 8-ounce short, round glass is used for holding ice and spirits, as well as some cocktails, most notably the Old Fashioned.

Poco/Hurricane: A large, 14- to 20-ounce curved and stemmed glass, designed to look like a hurricane lamp, used for serving the Hurricane cocktail or blended or frozen drinks.

Rocks: See Old Fashioned.

CHAPTER ★ ONE

A.C. **001** A.C.

Mark Twain's famous quip **"SOMETIMES TOO MUCH TO DRINK IS BARELY ENOUGH"** could be the credo of the South—whether it's iced tea or an ice-cold cocktail, Southerners love to wash the day down with a delicious drink. From Mardi Gras to the Kentucky Derby to lounging on a porch swing on a sweltering summer day, drinking is a sign of hospitality, celebration, and day-to-day enjoyment, and like the food of the South, the region's drinks are full of character and flavor. The South brought us many of America's most venerable classic cocktails, such as the Sazerac, Vieux Carré, and Mint Julep, and Southern bartenders take pride in that history, crafting cocktails that reflect a sense of past and present culture. And with a heritage that includes the production of some of the world's best cocktail ingredients—from Kentucky bourbon to Georgia peaches—it's no wonder that the South provides one of the best opportunities in the country to truly experience the taste of place.

SEELBACH COCKTAIL

Kentucky is home to the world's finest bourbons and, as such, is naturally the source of inspiration for many of the most beloved whiskey-based cocktails. Named after the famous hotel in Louisville, this classic cocktail remains as popular today as it was back in the early twentieth century. The Seelbach fortifies a backbone of bourbon with a touch of Cointreau, two types of bitters, and a splash of sparkling wine for a sophisticated sipper that will transport you to a more genteel time and place.

SERVES
★
1

TOOLS

MIXING GLASS
BARSPOON
FINE-MESH
STRAINER

GLASS

FLUTE

GARNISH

LEMON TWIST

2 ounces bourbon

½ ounce Cointreau

7 dashes of Angostura bitters

7 dashes of Peychaud's bitters

Ice cubes

4 to 5 ounces Champagne or other sparkling wine

Combine the bourbon, Cointreau, and Angostura and Peychaud's bitters in a mixing glass, add ice, and stir until chilled. Strain into a flute. Top with the Champagne and garnish with the lemon twist.

FARMER'S CHOICE

With its proximity to the Caribbean islands and large Cuban, Dominican, and Puerto Rican populations, Miami is fully infused with the flavors and culture of rum. Classic rum cocktails, such as Mojitos and Cuba Libres, can be found on menus across the city, and at the Florida Room in the Delano Hotel, bartender Gabriel Orta mixes up an array of creative rum-based recipes, including this deliciously refreshing sipper combining aged rum with red bell peppers and a generous helping of citrus, another essential flavor of southern Florida food and drink.

SERVES
★
1

TOOLS

MUDDLER
COCKTAIL
SHAKER
FINE-MESH
STRAINER

GLASS

HIGHBALL

GARNISH

GRAPEFRUIT
PEEL
RED BELL
PEPPER RING

2 chunks fresh red bell pepper, seeded and deribbed

1¾ ounces aged rum

1 ounce fresh grapefruit juice

½ ounce fresh lemon juice

¾ ounce sugarcane syrup (see Tip)

Dash of rhubarb bitters

Ice cubes

Muddle the bell pepper in a cocktail shaker. Add the rum, grapefruit juice, lemon juice, sugarcane syrup, and bitters and shake well with ice. Double strain into an ice-filled highball glass. Garnish with the grapefruit peel and bell pepper ring.

GABRIEL ORTA
FLORIDA ROOM, MIAMI, FLORIDA

A.C.001
TIP
Sugarcane syrup is a thick, intensely sweet syrup made from sugarcane juice. It's available in specialty grocery stores and online.

ACROSS THE BOARD

There are few things as quintessentially Kentucky as the Mint Julep, and right in the heart of bourbon country, Jennifer Pittman of Louisville's Proof on Main puts a modern twist on the classic cocktail. With a traditional base of mint and bourbon, she showcases the fresh, sweet flavor of strawberries, which grow abundantly throughout Kentucky. "One of my favorite things about summer in Kentucky is the revealing of the first bunches of fresh, ripe, red strawberries," Pittman says. "These tiny fruits pack a whole lot of flavor, and when combined with mint and rhubarb, they make a delicious concoction. Balsamic vinegar is the perfect addition, with its sweet-tart finish. The result will make even the most traditional Julep connoisseurs go back for a second helping."

SERVES
★
1

TOOLS

MUDDLER
MIXING GLASS
BARSPOON
FINE-MESH
STRAINER

GLASS

JULEP CUP

GARNISH

MINT SPRIG

8 to 10 mint leaves

2 fresh strawberries, hulled

Dash of rhubarb bitters

1 teaspoon granulated sugar

½ teaspoon quality balsamic vinegar

2½ ounces bourbon (preferably sweeter bourbon, such as Old Weller or Van Winkle)

Ice cubes, for mixing

Crushed ice, for serving

Place the mint leaves in a Julep cup and lightly bruise with a muddler. Set aside. In a mixing glass, muddle the strawberries with the bitters, sugar, and vinegar. Add the bourbon, fill the glass with ice cubes, and stir until chilled. Double strain the mixture over the mint leaves in the Julep cup. Add plenty of crushed ice and garnish with the mint sprig.

JENNIFER PITTMAN
PROOF ON MAIN, LOUISVILLE, KENTUCKY

Take care not to overmuddle the mint leaves, as they will become bitter if bruised too much. Instead, you want to lightly press the leaves with a muddler or the back of a spoon to gently release the herb's oils.

BIG BAY STORM

If you've ever visited or lived in North Carolina, you've surely had the pleasure of tasting Cheerwine, a cherry-flavored cola that's been produced in Salisbury, North Carolina, since 1917 and is considered a statewide treasure. Locals use Cheerwine in everything from ice cream to barbecue sauce, and at Crook's Corner in Chapel Hill, you can find it in cocktails, including this one by Shannon Healy, which balances the sweetness of the soda, rum, and pineapple juice with the bitterness of Campari and the tang of lime juice.

SERVES
★
1

TOOLS

COCKTAIL
SHAKER
FINE-MESH
STRAINER

GLASS

COLLINS

GARNISH

ORANGE WHEEL

1¼ ounces Gosling's rum

¾ ounce Campari

¾ ounce fresh lemon juice

¾ ounce pineapple juice

Ice cubes

1 ounce Cheerwine soda

→ Combine the rum, Campari, lemon juice, and pineapple juice in a cocktail shaker, add ice, and shake vigorously. Strain into an ice-filled Collins glass. Top with the Cheerwine, stir to combine, and garnish with the orange wheel.

SHANNON HEALY
CROOK'S CORNER, CHAPEL HILL, NORTH CAROLINA

CHARLESTON TEA PUNCH

Charleston, South Carolina, was the first place to grow tea in America, and because sweetened iced tea is a staple of low-country life, it makes sense that it would find its way into Southern cocktails. Using a raspberry-flavored black tea from the Charleston Tea Plantation—the only commercial tea plantation in America—Charleston bartender Jason Hall puts a delicious twist on the classic Planter's Punch in this flavorful concoction. "I get asked to make this drink quite a bit," he says, making this Southern cocktail "second only to the Mint Julep."

SERVES
★
1

TOOLS

COCKTAIL SHAKER
FINE-MESH STRAINER

GLASS

COCKTAIL

GARNISH

ORANGE SLICE
2 FRESH RASPBERRIES

1 ounce light rum

1 ounce dark rum

1 ounce Cointreau

1 ounce Raspberry Tea Simple Syrup (facing page)

1 ounce fresh lime juice

1 teaspoon raspberry preserves

1 teaspoon orange preserves

Dash of Angostura bitters

Ice cubes

Combine the light and dark rums, Cointreau, simple syrup, lime juice, raspberry and orange preserves, and bitters in a cocktail shaker, add ice, and shake well. Double strain into a chilled cocktail glass. Garnish with the orange slice and raspberries, skewered on a cocktail pick.

JASON HALL
CHARLESTON GRILL, CHARLESTON, SOUTH CAROLINA

RASPBERRY TEA SIMPLE SYRUP MAKES ABOUT 1½ CUPS

1½ teaspoons loose-leaf
American Classic Rockville
Raspberry Tea or other
raspberry-flavored black tea

1 cup boiling water

1 cup granulated sugar

Steep the tea in the water for 2 minutes. Strain the tea into a small saucepan, add the sugar, and bring to a simmer over medium-low heat. Continue to simmer, stirring slowly, until the sugar is dissolved, 2 to 3 minutes. Remove from the heat and let cool before transferring to a clean glass bottle. Cover and refrigerate for up to 2 weeks.

COMFORTABLY OLD FASHIONED

Bartender Lu Brow is a local celebrity in the Big Easy, mixing up regional favorites at Café Adelaide's legendary Swizzle Stick Bar. One of her most popular recipes is the Comfortably Old Fashioned, a clever twist on the classic bourbon-based Old Fashioned cocktail. Instead of bourbon, Brow uses Southern Comfort, a New Orleans original that blends whiskey with fruit and spices. And for a final touch, she garnishes the drink with a housemade brandied cherry.

SERVES
★
1

TOOLS

MUDDLER
BARSPOON

GLASS

OLD FASHIONED

GARNISH

BRANDIED
CHERRY
(RECIPE
FOLLOWS)

1 orange wheel, halved	2 ounces Southern Comfort
½ barspoon granulated sugar	Ice chunk
2 dashes of Angostura bitters	

➤ Muddle the orange wheel, sugar, and bitters in an Old Fashioned glass. Add the Southern Comfort and stir. Add a large chunk of ice and garnish with a brandied cherry.

LU BROW
SWIZZLE STICK BAR, NEW ORLEANS, LOUISIANA

LU'S BRANDIED CHERRIES MAKES 2 CUPS

1 pound sweet cherries	1 cinnamon stick
½ cup granulated sugar	Pinch of freshly grated nutmeg
½ cup water	1 teaspoon pure vanilla extract
2 teaspoons fresh lemon juice	1 cup brandy

➤ Wash and pit the cherries. In a small saucepan, combine the sugar, water, lemon juice, cinnamon stick, nutmeg, and vanilla and bring to a rolling boil. When the liquid begins to boil, reduce the heat to medium. Add the cherries and simmer for 5 to 7 minutes. Remove from the heat, stir in the brandy, and let cool. Transfer the cherries and their cooking liquid to a clean jar and refrigerate, uncovered, until the cherries are cool to the touch. Cover tightly and refrigerate for up to 2 weeks.

COPPER FOX COOLER

Virginia has a long history of distilling, with George Washington getting into the business of making whiskey at Mount Vernon in 1797. More than two hundred years later, the Copper Fox Distillery, in Sperryville, Virginia, keeps the tradition alive, producing a variety of small-batch whiskey. Created by native Virginian Todd Thrasher of PX in Alexandria, this recipe combines Copper Fox's single-malt whiskey with locally grown blackberries and an herbal lemonade for a deliciously nuanced cocktail that would make Virginia's whiskey-loving forefathers proud.

SERVES
★
1

TOOLS

MUDDLER
COCKTAIL
SHAKER
FINE-MESH
STRAINER

GLASS

HIGHBALL

GARNISH

SAGE SPRIG
(SEE TIP)

2 fresh blackberries

1½ ounces Wasmund's single-malt whiskey

3 ounces Sage Lemonade (facing page)

Ice cubes

1 ounce soda water

Muddle the blackberries in a cocktail shaker. Add the whiskey and lemonade and shake well with ice. Double strain into an ice-filled highball glass. Top with the soda water and garnish with the sage sprig.

TODD THRASHER
PX, ALEXANDRIA, VIRGINIA

To release the aroma of the sage garnish, place the herb in the palm of one hand and smack it with the other.

SAGE LEMONADE MAKES ABOUT 5 CUPS

1 cup granulated sugar	4 cups water
4 fresh sage leaves, crushed	1 cup fresh lemon juice

→ Combine the sugar, sage leaves, and ½ cup of the water in a small saucepan and bring to a boil. Reduce the heat to medium-low and simmer, stirring slowly until the sugar is dissolved, 2 to 3 minutes. Remove from the heat and let cool to room temperature. Cover and refrigerate until chilled. In a pitcher, stir together the chilled sage syrup, the lemon juice, and the remaining 3½ cups of water. Cover and refrigerate for up to 2 days.

DIXIE CUP

"The Dixie Cup is our homage to the South in general and Atlanta in particular," says Atlanta bartender Timothy Faulkner, who created this charming cocktail as a testament to the beauty of simplicity and lauds it as "simultaneously sharp and palatable, recognizable and unfamiliar." Both Four Roses bourbon and Red Rock ginger ale originate from Reconstruction-era Atlanta, and sugar and citrus are staple ingredients of Southern cooking. Together, they create a perfectly refined cocktail with a refreshing kick of spice—very Southern indeed.

SERVES
★
1

TOOLS

MIXING GLASS
BARSPOON
FINE-MESH
STRAINER

GLASS

HIGHBALL

GARNISH

LIME TWIST

2 ounces Four Roses Yellow Label bourbon

1½ ounces Red Rock ginger ale or other spicy ginger ale

½ ounce sugarcane syrup (see Tip, page 19)

Ice cubes

Combine the bourbon, ginger ale, and sugarcane syrup in an ice-filled mixing glass and stir gently. Strain into an ice-filled highball glass. Rub the lime twist around the rim of the glass before dropping it into the cocktail.

TIMOTHY VICTOR FAULKNER
SAUCED, ATLANTA, GEORGIA

KELSO DAIQUIRI

Smack-dab in the middle of Tennessee whiskey country and literally down the road from Jack Daniel's, sits Prichards' Distillery, quietly crafting rum, of all things, in the tiny town of Kelso. And if it seems odd to find a traditionally tropical spirit being produced in a landocked Southern state, Josh Habiger of the Patterson House in Nashville has taken things a step further with the bar's Kelso Daiquiri. "I wanted to have something on our menu that showcased the unique flavor of Prichards' and also could teach Nashville what a Daiquiri is," he says. Indeed, it's a perfectly charming Southern twist on a classic beach cocktail.

SERVES
★
1

TOOLS

COCKTAIL SHAKER
FINE-MESH STRAINER

GLASS

COUPE

GARNISH

LIME WHEEL

2 ounces Prichards' Crystal rum | ¾ ounce Simple Syrup (recipe follows)
¾ ounce fresh lime juice | Ice cubes

➤ Combine the rum, lime juice, and simple syrup in a cocktail shaker, add ice, and shake well. Strain into a chilled coupe. Float the lime wheel on the drink's surface or twist it onto a skewer.

JOSH HABIGER
THE PATTERSON HOUSE, NASHVILLE, TENNESSEE

SIMPLE SYRUP MAKES ABOUT 1½ CUPS

1 cup water | 1 cup granulated sugar

➤ Combine the water and sugar in a small saucepan and bring to a boil, stirring constantly. Reduce the heat to medium-low and simmer, stirring slowly, until the sugar is dissolved, 2 to 3 minutes. Remove from the heat and let cool to room temperature. Transfer to a clean glass container, cover, and refrigerate for up to 2 weeks.

PIG ON THE PORCH

Greenville's American Grocery Restaurant showcases locally grown and sustainably raised ingredients in both its food and cocktail menus, and few ingredients represent the heart of South Carolina cuisine more than pork. "Ask any native and they'll tell you that the pig *rules!*" says co-owner and sommelier Darlene Clarke. "From the myriad styles of barbeque to the simple pleasure of farmhouse sausage, the pig is the unofficial South Carolina mascot." To celebrate the pig's place of honor in the state's cuisine, she combines bacon-infused bourbon with locally made Blenheim ginger ale for a quintessential Palmetto State cocktail. "Not for the faint of heart," Clarke says, "this ginger ale packs a spicy kick that, when combined with the bacon bourbon, delivers a smoky yet clean and refreshing libation to relieve the sweltering heat of the South."

SERVES
★
1

TOOLS

BARSPOON

GLASS

COLLINS

GARNISH

CANDIED
BACON
(SEE NOTE)
1 PORK RIND

2 ounces Bacon Bourbon (page 36)

4 ounces Blenheim ginger ale, medium heat (see Tip)

Ice cubes

Combine the bourbon and ginger ale in an ice-filled Collins glass and stir to combine. Garnish with the candied bacon and pork rind.

DARLENE AND JOE CLARKE
AMERICAN GROCERY, GREENVILLE, SOUTH CAROLINA

To make the candied bacon, drizzle cooked bacon strips with maple syrup or Simple Syrup (page 33). Use immediately (it will be sticky, so be careful handling it).

Blenheim ginger ale comes in two styles: medium and hot. They're both spicy, but the intense heat of the hot version can overwhelm other flavors, so for cocktails, medium usually works best.

BACON BOURBON MAKES 1 LITER

| 1 liter bourbon | Eight 1-inch-thick strips good-quality, hardwood-smoked bacon, or enough to render ½ cup of bacon fat |

Pour the bourbon into a nonreactive container, preferably glass. Save the bourbon bottle to serve and store the finished bacon bourbon. In a skillet, fry the bacon. Reserve ½ cup of rendered fat, allowing it to cool but not congeal. (Set the fried bacon aside for the garnish or another use.) Once the rendered fat has cooled slightly, pour it into the bourbon. Cover and store at room temperature in a cool, dark place for 1 day and then refrigerate for 2 more, allowing the bacon fat to congeal on the surface. Skim off the congealed bacon fat and discard. Strain the infused bourbon through a cheesecloth-lined strainer to remove any smaller bits of fat. Using a funnel, pour the bacon-infused bourbon into the original bourbon bottle and store in a cool, dark place.

LA VIDA NARANJA

Meyer lemons thrive in the subtropical Louisiana climate, and they make the perfect ingredient for citrus-forward cocktails. With less acidity than traditional lemons and a sweet, concentrated lemon flavor, juicy Meyers (which are believed to be a cross between a Valencia orange and a lemon) shine in this bright, nuanced recipe from New Orleans bartender Danny Valdez, which marries the sweet, rich flavors of Grand Marnier and apricot liqueur with the acidity of Meyer lemons and the bitterness of orange bitters. A delicious ode to the Crescent City.

SERVES
★
1

TOOLS

COCKTAIL SHAKER
FINE-MESH STRAINER

GLASS

COUPE
××OR××
COCKTAIL

1½ ounces Grand Marnier

½ ounce apricot liqueur

1 ounce fresh Meyer lemon juice

¾ ounce Simple Syrup (page 33)

2 dashes of Bitter Truth orange bitters or Regans' orange bitters

Ice cubes

→ Combine the Grand Marnier, apricot liqueur, lemon juice, simple syrup, and bitters in a cocktail shaker, add ice, and shake well. Strain into a chilled coupe.

DANNY VALDEZ
CURE, NEW ORLEANS, LOUISIANA

SINISTER PROPOSAL

Franciscan monks introduced peaches to Georgia in the sixteenth century, and today the Peach State produces about 2.6 million bushels annually. Come summertime in Georgia, the sweet, juicy fruit shows up in just about everything, from cobblers to cocktails. At Restaurant Eugene in Atlanta, Nick Hearin highlights peaches in his "sinister" sipper, making housemade peach amaretto the star of the show. What more could you ask for than a cocktail that allows you to eat a peach and find a use for the pit when you're done?

SERVES
★
1

TOOLS

MIXING GLASS
BARSPOON
FINE-MESH
STRAINER

GLASS

CORDIAL

GARNISH

ORANGE PEEL

1 ounce Cynar

1 ounce Peach Amaretto (facing page)

2 dashes of Regans' orange bitters

Ice cubes

Combine the Cynar, amaretto, and bitters in a mixing glass, add ice, and stir until chilled. Strain into a cordial glass and garnish with the orange peel.

NICK HEARIN
RESTAURANT EUGENE, ATLANTA, GEORGIA

PEACH AMARETTO MAKES 750 ML

2 pounds peach pits

750 ml VS cognac

1 cinnamon stick

2 cloves

Pinch of sassafras

1 cup turbinado sugar

1 cup water

➤ To prepare the peach pits, dry them on a towel. Preheat the broiler. Crack the dried pits open using a wedge and a mallet. Remove the kernels and roast them under the broiler for 1 minute. Remove from the oven and let cool.

➤ Pour the cognac into a large glass jar. Add the peach cooled kernels, cover, and store at room temperature in a cool, dark place for 3 weeks. Add the cinnamon stick, cloves, and sassafras, cover, and allow to infuse in a cool, dark place for 1 week more. Carefully strain the infused spirit through a strainer lined with a double layer of cheesecloth into a clean glass bottle. Add the sugar and water and stir until most of the sugar is dissolved. Let sit for 1 week before use.

CHAPTER ★ TWO

NORTHEAST

A.C. **002** A.C.

The Northeast is where it all began—the first battles, the first declarations, the first forays into democracy. EVEN THE BIRTH OF COCKTAILS CAN BE TRACED BACK TO THE NORTHEAST, the cradle of the United States. So it's no surprise that its residents take pride in their history and work hard to keep their traditions alive, from a New Jersey distillery that's been making applejack for 300 years to Cape Cod cranberry bogs with vines more than 150 years old. The bartenders in this region offer a link between the past and present, taking advantage of indigenous fruits and traditional products to make inventive cocktails with true character. Where else can you get a cutting-edge drink made with produce from centuries-old farms and spirits from distillers reviving centuries-old traditions? Bartenders take classic cocktails, born here generations ago, and reinvigorate them with inspired flavors and handcrafted ingredients. It's the blending of old and new, the reverence for the past mixed with the ingenuity of today, that makes the Northeast's cocktails worth raising a glass to.

WARD EIGHT

This old-school cocktail, a relative of the Whiskey Sour, is thought to have been first created at Boston's Locke-Ober Café in the 1898 celebration of Democrat Martin Lomasney's win as the city's eighth-ward representative to the Massachusetts General Court (the eighth ward was believed to have tipped the election results). Lomasney was famous for saying "Never write if you can speak; never speak if you can nod; never nod if you can wink." The Ward Eight cocktail embraces this philosophy of discretion by using just the right amount of spice from the whiskey, sweetness from the grenadine, and tartness from the lemon juice. If ever there were a classic cocktail Boston should be proud to call its own, it is this one.

SERVES
★
1

TOOLS

COCKTAIL
SHAKER
FINE-MESHED
STRAINER

GLASS

COCKTAIL

GARNISH

MARASCA
CHERRY

2 ounces rye whiskey

¾ ounce fresh lemon juice

¾ ounce fresh orange juice

1 teaspoon grenadine

Ice cubes

→ Combine the whiskey, lemon juice, orange juice, and grenadine in a cocktail shaker, add ice, and shake well. Strain into a chilled cocktail glass and garnish with a skewered Marasca cherry.

BOSTON BOG

Of all the indigenous flora of North America, only three native fruits are commercially grown, and one is the cranberry. Though the berries are cultivated in several regions around the United States and Canada, nowhere are they more intertwined with a state's economic, agricultural, and social history than in Massachusetts, where Native Americans first taught Colonial Americans what to do with the nutritious berries and where cranberry cultivation was born. Fourteen thousand acres of commercial cranberry bogs can now be found on the sandy shores of Cape Cod, where some of the bushes are more than 150 years old. To capture the history and flavor of this special berry, Boston bartender Misty Kalkofen mixes fresh cranberries with Jamaican rum, that other Colonial American staple. For spicy depth, she adds housemade ginger syrup, balanced by a kiss of sweet apricot liqueur.

SERVES
★
1

TOOLS

MUDDLER
COCKTAIL
SHAKER
FINE-MESH
STRAINER

GLASS

COCKTAIL

GARNISH

1-INCH-BY-
2-INCH
PIECE OF
ORANGE PEEL

6 fresh cranberries or ½ ounce cranberry juice

1½ ounces Appleton Estate Reserve Jamaica rum

½ ounce Rothman & Winter apricot liqueur

½ ounce Ginger Syrup (page 46)

½ ounce fresh lemon juice

Ice cubes

If using fresh cranberries, muddle them in a cocktail shaker. Add the rum, apricot liqueur, ginger syrup, and lemon juice (and the cranberry juice, if using) and shake well with ice. Double strain into a chilled cocktail glass. Garnish with the orange peel, twisting it over the drink to release the oils.

MISTY KALKOFEN
DRINK, BOSTON, MASSACHUSETTS

GINGER SYRUP MAKES ABOUT 1½ CUPS

1 cup water

1 cup Demerara sugar

1 cup diced fresh ginger, skin on

→ Combine the water and sugar in a medium saucepan and bring to a boil. Reduce the heat to medium-low and simmer, stirring slowly until the sugar is dissolved, 2 to 3 minutes. Remove from the heat and let cool to room temperature. In a blender or food processor, purée the ginger with the sugar mixture, then strain through a fine-mesh strainer into a clean glass container. Cover and refrigerate for up to 2 weeks.

BLACKLOCK'S DEMISE

From the earliest days of the United States, Vermont grew so many apples it was said that cider flowed more freely than water. It was even used as currency for trading. So it's no surprise that the state is still home to some of the best apples and hard apple cider in the country—and that both often find their way into cocktails in bars around the state. At the Up Top Tavern south of Burlington, bartender Jeff Becher uses local Woodchuck cider to add crisp apple flavor to his drinks. Here, he pairs the cider with port, creating a drink that evokes spiced pies and fall in Vermont.

SERVES
★
1

TOOLS

COCKTAIL SHAKER
FINE-MESH STRAINER

GLASS

COCKTAIL

GARNISH

APPLE SLICE

½ ounce port

½ ounce apricot brandy

1 ounce pineapple juice

3 ounces Woodchuck Amber hard cider

Ice cubes

Combine the port, brandy, pineapple juice, and hard cider in a cocktail shaker with ice and shake well. Strain into a cocktail glass. Garnish by perching the apple slice on the rim.

JEFF BECHER
UP TOP TAVERN, VERGENNES, VERMONT

CAMDEN HIKE

Maine's sixty thousand acres of wild blueberries are a gift to the nation's northern-most residents. Blueberries thrive in the region's acidic soils and weather the harsh winters like champs, enabling the area to offer up the intensely flavorful, versatile, and nutritious berries for thousands of years and counting. The first cultivated blueberries were transplanted from the wild, and now Maine is the largest producer in the world. Bartender Tom Laslavic pays tribute to these gems and the flavors of his home state with this sparkling, berry-laden drink. "These are ingredients one may find during a country walk in midcoast Maine," he says. He also draws inspiration from local distiller Cold River Vodka, which makes vodka with Maine-grown potatoes.

SERVES
★
1

TOOLS

COCKTAIL SHAKER
FINE-MESH STRAINER

GLASS

DOUBLE OLD FASHIONED

GARNISH

1 PIECE OF THICK LEMON PEEL
1 FRESH BLACKBERRY
1 FRESH BLUEBERRY

---

1 ounce strained blackberry purée (see Note)

1 ounce strained blueberry purée (see Note)

1 ounce Maine wildflower honey syrup (see Note)

2 ounces Cold River vodka

¼ ounce crème de cassis

¾ ounce lemon juice

Ice cubes

3 to 4 ounces soda water

➤ Combine both berry purées and the honey syrup, vodka, crème de cassis, and lemon juice in a cocktail shaker with ice and shake well. Strain into a double Old Fashioned glass. Top with the soda water and garnish with the lemon peel and berries, skewered on a cocktail pick.

TOM LASLAVIC
NATALIE'S RESTAURANT, CAMDEN HARBOUR INN, CAMDEN, MAINE

A.C.002
NOTE

To make the berry purées, place 1 cup of fresh or frozen blackberries in a blender or food processor and process until puréed. Strain through a fine-mesh strainer and set aside. Repeat with the blueberries.

To make the honey syrup, in a heatproof container, mix at least 1 tablespoon of Maine wildflower honey with an equal amount of warm water. Stir until blended.

COMFORT COFFEE

Back in the seventeenth century, New York was one of the first states to sow the seeds of American coffee culture. Today, coffee remains a year-round staple for New Yorkers, who can now take advantage of plenty of locally roasted brews. Among New York's finest homegrown roasters is Gimme! Coffee, which operates a roastery and cafés in Ithaca, along with cafés in Brooklyn and Manhattan. In 2004, Felicia's Atomic Lounge opened next door to the original Gimme! roastery, and ever since, the two have been collaborating on all sorts of coffee-based cocktails. Created by Felicia's bartender Leah Houghtaling, this concoction combines Gimme! Coffee's fresh-roasted beans with bourbon and a spiced simple syrup for a truly decadent winter warmer. Whip up a mug of this, and those icy winter winds won't stand a chance.

SERVES
★
1

TOOLS

BARSPOON

GLASS

MUG

GARNISH

ORANGE TWIST

---

1 ounce bourbon

1 ounce Felicia's Comfort Syrup (facing page)

6 ounces fresh, hot French-pressed coffee (see Tip)

Combine the bourbon and syrup in a mug and stir until blended. Add the hot coffee, stir, and garnish with the orange twist.

LEAH HOUGHTALING
FELICIA'S ATOMIC LOUNGE, ITHACA, NEW YORK

This recipe works especially well with coffee from Mexico or El Salvador, which has bold and chocolaty flavors that riff beautifully off the round, rich notes of bourbon.

FELICIA'S COMFORT SYRUP MAKES ABOUT 1 CUP

¾ cup fresh orange juice without pulp

½ cup granulated sugar

⅛ teaspoon ground cloves

1½ teaspoons cardamom seeds

→ Combine the orange juice, sugar, cloves, and cardamom in a small saucepan. Cook over medium-low heat, stirring slowly until the syrup is hot and the sugar is dissolved; do not boil. Remove from the heat. Cover and let sit for 20 minutes. Strain into a clean glass container, cover, and refrigerate for up to 2 weeks.

CORDOVA COCKTAIL

Southwark Restaurant in Philadelphia prides itself on perfectly executed classic cocktails, but bartender and co-owner Kip Waide puts his own spin on things by using local spirits whenever he can. In this timeless drink from the 1934 edition of William "Cocktail" Boothby's *World's Drinks and How to Mix Them*, Waide uses Vieux Carré absinthe and Philadelphia-made Bluecoat gin. Distilled five times from rye, wheat, barley, and corn in hand-hammered copper pot stills, then flavored with juniper berries and citrus peels, the smooth gin pairs perfectly with the absinthe and sweet vermouth.

SERVES
★
1

TOOLS

COCKTAIL
SHAKER
FINE-MESH
STRAINER

GLASS

COCKTAIL

1½ ounces Bluecoat gin

¾ ounce sweet vermouth

2 or 3 dashes of
Vieux Carré absinthe

¼ ounce heavy cream

Ice cubes

Combine the gin, vermouth, absinthe, and cream in a cocktail shaker, add ice, and shake well. Strain into a chilled cocktail glass.

KIP WAIDE
SOUTHWARK RESTAURANT, PHILADELPHIA, PENNSYLVANIA

THE OLD NEIGHBORHOOD

New Yorkers love to debate the origin of egg cream, the soda fountain classic that's become as iconic as Times Square. But even though its birth is shrouded in mystery, everyone agrees on three things: there should be no eggs and no cream, and you must use Fox's U-Bet chocolate syrup. Since the history of egg creams is inextricably linked with the candy shops of Brooklyn, it's especially fitting that Brooklyn bartender Damon Boelte has become a big fan, using egg creams as the base for a spirited drink spiked with premium rum. "Egg creams begin to separate when left sitting around for too long," he says. "That's why there's not much alcohol in this drink. It's meant to be drunk quickly on the hottest of Brooklyn days." Think of it as chocolate milk that's fizzed up and frothy with a blast of seltzer, plus a splash of booze to make it all grown-up.

SERVES

1

TOOLS

BARSPOON

GLASS

COLLINS

1 ounce Fox's U-Bet chocolate syrup

¾ ounce spiced rum

¾ ounce dark Jamaican rum

3 ounces very cold whole milk

3 ounces very cold soda water

Combine the chocolate syrup, spiced rum, dark rum, and milk in a Collins glass. With a barspoon, beat the syrup against the side of the glass until it's completely mixed in with the other ingredients. Top with the soda water and stir gently.

DAMON BOELTE
PRIME MEATS, BROOKLYN, NEW YORK

MAPLE SYRUP TODDY

Perhaps the earliest form of a cocktail, toddies were created as a way to chase away the chill and offer relief from colds and flu. A couple hundred years later, we're still drinking them for the same reasons, though bartenders like John Ginnetti are upping the ante with premium spirits and creative combinations, making drinks you definitely want to sip while you're hale and hearty. For this New England–inspired version, the owner of 116 Crown in Connecticut reaches for Laird's applejack, which has been made in nearby New Jersey since the 1700s. Then he sweetens the mix with pure maple syrup, one of the state's biggest crops. Instead of adding traditional spices, he uses sweet vermouth and Averna, an Italian amaro, to give the drink aromatic complexity.

SERVES
★
1

TOOLS

BARSPOON

GLASS

MUG

GARNISH

1-INCH-BY-
2-INCH
PIECE OF
LEMON PEEL

2 ounces applejack

1 ounce sweet vermouth

1 ounce Averna

1 teaspoon Grade B maple syrup (see Tip)

3 ounces hot water

Combine the applejack, vermouth, Averna, and maple syrup in a mug and stir until blended. Add the hot water and stir again. Garnish with the lemon peel, twisting it over the drink to release the oils.

JOHN GINNETTI
116 CROWN, NEW HAVEN, CONNECTICUT

A.C.002
TIP

Maple syrup produced in the United States is usually labeled as Grade A or Grade B. Grade A syrup comes from maple trees tapped in early spring and is lighter in color and milder in flavor. This drink is best when made with darker, more robustly flavored Grade B syrup, which comes from trees tapped later in the season.

MINT APPLE CRISP

In the early 1900s, New York state had more than one thousand stills on local farms. Then Prohibition started in 1920, spelling the legal end for the country's distilleries, both large and small. It took eighty-three years for a New York distillery to pick up the torch, but finally, in 2003, Tuthilltown Spirits launched, becoming New York's first small-batch whiskey distiller since the "Noble Experiment" put everyone out of business. When New York City bartenders Jim Meehan and Karen Fu set out to craft a cocktail that honors their home state, which happens to be the second largest producer of apples in the country, they reached for Tuthilltown's Heart of the Hudson vodka, made with apple cider from local orchards. Muddled Granny Smith apple plus fresh mint and saké give the drink a deliciously fresh, green-apple crispness.

SERVES
★
1

TOOLS

MUDDLER
MIXING GLASS
BARSPOON
FINE-MESH
STRAINER

GLASS

COUPE

GARNISH

4 THIN SLICES
GRANNY SMITH
APPLE

Three ¼-inch-thick slices Granny Smith apple

¼ ounce Simple Syrup (page 33)

2 fresh mint leaves

2 ounces Heart of the Hudson apple vodka

1 ounce junmai saké

Ice cubes

Muddle the apple slices and simple syrup in a mixing glass. Add the mint leaves and press lightly with the muddler. Add the vodka, saké, and ice, and stir until chilled. Double strain into a chilled coupe and garnish with the fanned apple slices.

KAREN FU AND JIM MEEHAN
PDT, NEW YORK, NEW YORK

CHAPTER ★ THREE

MIDWEST

A.C. **003** A.C.

The Midwest is all about comfort, especially when it comes to eating and drinking. Brandy Alexander, anyone? Tom and Jerry? **APPLES, WALNUTS, AND CHERRIES ARE JUST A FEW OF THE MANY MIDWESTERN FLAVORS THAT WARM OUR SOULS,** and the cocktails that come out of the region make the most of them. The melting pot of cultures that found their way to this part of country—Scandinavian, German, English, and Irish, to name a few—has inspired cocktails that may seem simple at first glance but are deceptively complex and nuanced. And as it turns out, the Midwest is also a hot-bed of craft distilling (and brewing, of course), with everything from absinthe to gin to whiskey being produced throughout the area. Most Midwesterners would be more than happy to have you crack open a cold beer for them, but whip up a brandy cocktail, and you might have a friend for life.

BITTER BRANCH

Minnesotans, who have an abundance of walnut trees in their state, know that green walnuts are best used for making nocino, an Italian bittersweet walnut liqueur that is versatile and decadent in cocktails. Created by Pip Hanson of Marvel Bar in Minneapolis, this simple yet flavorful cocktail makes a great digestif to cap off a heavy dinner on a cold Midwestern night. The spicy rye whiskey is a perfect counterpart to the nuttiness of the nocino, and the chocolaty character of the Cynar blends beautifully with the surprising addition of sea salt water.

SERVES
★
1

TOOLS

MIXING GLASS
BARSPOON
FINE-MESH
STRAINER

GLASS

OLD FASHIONED

GARNISH

ORANGE TWIST
CANDIED
WALNUT
(PAGE 62)

3 or 4 drops of sea salt water (see Note)

3 ounces rye whiskey

1 ounce Cynar

½ ounce nocino or nocello

Ice cubes

Combine the sea salt water, whiskey, Cynar, and nocino in a mixing glass, add ice, and stir until chilled. Strain into an Old Fashioned glass and garnish with the orange twist and candied walnut.

PIP HANSON
MARVEL BAR, MINNEAPOLIS, MINNESOTA

To make the sea salt water, in a mug, stir 2 tablespoons of sea salt into ½ cup of boiling water, stirring until dissolved. Chill well before use.

CANDIED WALNUTS MAKES ¾ CUP

¾ cup unsalted raw walnut halves

¼ cup granulated sugar

Pinch of salt

Pinch of cayenne

→ Preheat the oven to 350 degrees F. Spread the walnuts evenly on a cookie sheet and bake until they are aromatic and begin to brown, 8 to 10 minutes. Remove from the oven and let cool.

→ In a small, heavy-bottomed saucepan over medium heat, cook the sugar, stirring continuously, until it melts into a syrup, 3 to 4 minutes. Immediately stir in the walnuts, quickly coating them evenly with the syrup before it cools. Scoop the nuts onto a cookie sheet, separating them as you go. Sprinkle them with the salt and cayenne and allow to cool completely. Store in an airtight container for up to 2 weeks.

CHERRY RUMBLE

East of the Mississippi grows a variety of wild, native cherry tree that has deep roots in our mixological past. Though its fruit is bitter to a fault, early settlers soon realized it made tasty wine and even better Cherry Bounce, a rum- or brandy-based cordial that many in the East still sip today. Inspired by these so-called rum cherry trees growing wild around Michigan, bartender David Turkel created a rum-based drink using two other native products: New Holland Distillery's Michigan Amber Freshwater rum and sparkling wine from L. Mawby Vineyards. And since Michigan is famous for its tart cherries, producing 75 percent of the country's crop, he opted to build the drink with them, creating a bright vinegary shrub to cut through the sweetness of the rum. "My thought is to celebrate regionalism," he says, "not just through the use of Michigan cherries, but with respect to some of the fine distillers, brewers, and vintners we're lucky to have in our state."

SERVES
★
1

TOOLS

COCKTAIL
SHAKER
FINE-MESH
STRAINER

GLASS

COLLINS

GARNISH

FRESH CHERRY

2 ounces New Holland's Michigan Amber Freshwater rum or Flor de Caña 4-year-old rum

1 ounce Michigan Tart Cherry Shrub (page 64; see Tip)

Dash of Fee Brothers cherry bitters

Ice cubes

2 ounces L. Mawby Blanc de Noir or Cava sparkling wine

Combine the rum, cherry shrub, and bitters in a cocktail shaker and dry shake. Strain into an ice-filled Collins glass. Top with the sparkling wine and garnish with the cherry.

DAVID TURKEL
VICEROY, GRAND RAPIDS, MICHIGAN

MICHIGAN TART CHERRY SHRUB MAKES ABOUT 2 CUPS

1 cup water

1 cup brown sugar

1 cup fresh or frozen pitted cherries

½ cup dried cherries

1 cup Champagne vinegar

→ Combine the water and brown sugar in a small saucepan and bring to a boil. Reduce the heat to medium-low and simmer, stirring slowly until the sugar is dissolved, 2 to 3 minutes. Add the fresh and dried cherries, cover, and simmer until the cherries begin to break down, 15 to 20 minutes. Add the vinegar and return to a boil. Remove from the heat and let cool. Strain into a clean glass container, cover, and refrigerate for up to 2 weeks.

If you don't want to make the cherry shrub from scratch, you can purchase a delicious bottled version online from Pennsylvania's Tait Farm Foods (see Resources, page 121).

ESCAPE FROM ALCATRAZ

Chicago was home to gangster Al Capone, who led a Prohibition-era alcohol smuggling and bootlegging ring and later went to prison at Alcatraz in San Francisco for tax evasion. Capone's favorite whiskey was said to be Templeton rye from Iowa, which was known during the time as the "Good Stuff," and legend has it that the whiskey even made it past the walls of Alcatraz. While the infamous gangster is long gone, Templeton lives on to this day, and this recipe from Chicago bartender Lynn House brings the story of Capone back to life.

SERVES

1

TOOLS

MUDDLER
COCKTAIL
SHAKER
FINE-MESH
STRAINER

GLASS

OLD FASHIONED

GARNISH

ORANGE SLICE

1 teaspoon peeled, grated fresh ginger

3 orange slices

½ ounce fresh lemon juice

1 ounce Cointreau

2 ounces Templeton rye whiskey

Ice cubes

Muddle the ginger, orange slices, and lemon juice in a cocktail shaker. Add the Cointreau and whiskey and shake well with ice. Double strain into an ice-filled Old Fashioned glass and garnish with the orange slice.

LYNN HOUSE
BLACKBIRD, CHICAGO, ILLINOIS

THE GOOD LIFE

Just a century ago, the city of Chicago boasted the second-largest population of Swedes in the world, next to Stockholm. Today, remnants of that Scandinavian heritage dot the Windy City at bakeries, bistros, and even a 24,000-square-foot cultural museum. Local distillery North Shore took note and began distilling their Scandinavian-inspired aquavit in 2006. Translating to "water of life," aquavit is a golden-hued, caraway-flavored spirit that was first popularized in the sixteenth century and is commonly consumed today throughout Scandinavia (and the midwestern United States) as a digestif. This cocktail, from Chicago-based bartender Benjamin Schiller, plays off aquavit's English translation and combines the spicy spirit with gingery Domaine de Canton, fresh lime, and Demerara syrup for a rich, food-friendly sipper. No lutefisk around? No worries. This cocktail complements all sorts of dishes, but to stay truly authentic, pair it with a heavy meal and a song, just like the Swedes would.

SERVES
★
1

TOOLS

COCKTAIL
SHAKER
FINE-MESH
STRAINER

GLASS

COUPE

GARNISH

ORANGE PEEL

1¾ ounces North Shore aquavit

1 ounce Domaine de Canton ginger liqueur

¾ ounce fresh lime juice

½ ounce Demerara Syrup (page 70)

10 drops of Regans' orange bitters

Ice cubes

→ Combine the aquavit, liqueur, lime juice, Demerara syrup, and bitters in a cocktail shaker with ice and shake well. Strain into a chilled coupe and garnish with the orange peel.

BENJAMIN SCHILLER
BOKA, CHICAGO, ILLINOIS

DEMERARA SYRUP MAKES ABOUT 2 CUPS

| 1 cup water | 2 cups Demerara sugar |

➤ Combine the water and sugar in a small saucepan and bring to a boil. Reduce the heat to medium-low and simmer, stirring slowly until the sugar is dissolved, 2 to 3 minutes. Remove from the heat and let cool to room temperature. Transfer to a clean glass container, cover, and refrigerate for up to 2 weeks.

ST. LOUIS SOUTHSIDE

Founded by colonial French traders nearly three centuries ago and sold to the United States by Napoleon Bonaparte in 1803, St. Louis is a city of rich culture and flavors that pay homage to its European heritage. Although oftentimes better known for its beer culture than cocktails (Anheuser-Busch embedded itself in the local economy back in 1852), things are shifting for this Midwestern city, with local bartenders looking toward quality ingredients for expertly prepared drinks. This libation from bartender Matt Seiter is a twist on the classic Southside cocktail, to which he adds Domaine de Canton ginger liqueur and a dash of absinthe in honor of the city's fertile French culture.

SERVES

★

1

TOOLS

MUDDLER
COCKTAIL SHAKER
FINE-MESH STRAINER

GLASS

POCO
××OR××
HURRICANE

GARNISH

MINT SPRIG

6 mint leaves

¾ ounce fresh lemon juice

¼ ounce Simple Syrup (page 33)

1½ ounces gin

¾ ounce Domaine de Canton ginger liqueur

Dash of absinthe

Ice cubes, for shaking

Crushed ice, for serving

1½ ounces tonic water

Muddle the mint leaves, lemon juice, and simple syrup in a cocktail shaker. Add the gin, ginger liqueur, and absinthe and shake well with ice cubes. Strain into a Poco glass filled with crushed ice. Top with the tonic water and garnish with the mint sprig.

MATT SEITER
SANCTUARIA, ST. LOUIS, MISSOURI

O'YAHDERHAY

This comforting cocktail combines many of Wisconsin's favorite culinary traditions in one recipe: brandy, kringle, ginger, and cranberries. Brandy is the official spirit of Wisconsin, so much so that 90 percent of the brandy that is consumed in the United States is imbibed in the Badger State. And though many outside of Wisconsin might never know it, Wisconsinites have a special affinity for ginger brandy, which they drink in shot glasses. The city of Racine also happens to be a mecca for kringle, a Danish pastry filled with nuts and preserved fruits, including cranberries, which are a must in this recipe. According to Milwaukee bartender Chad Doll, "The cranberry needs to be the representative fruit in the kringle syrup for this cocktail. Wisconsin produces more cranberries than any state in the nation and more than half for the entire world."

SERVES
★
1

TOOLS

COCKTAIL
SHAKER
FINE-MESH
STRAINER

GLASS

COUPE

GARNISH

5 DROPS OF
ANGOSTURA
BITTERS

1½ ounces Korbel brandy

1 ounce Kringle Syrup
(facing page)

1 ounce fresh lemon juice

½ ounce Punt e Mes vermouth

1 tablespoon fresh egg white
(see Tip)

Ice cubes

➤ Combine the brandy, kringle syrup, lemon juice, vermouth, and egg white in a cocktail shaker and dry shake for 15 seconds. Add the ice and shake vigorously for 20 seconds. Double strain into a chilled coupe and garnish with the bitters.

CHAD DOLL
HI HAT LOUNGE, MILWAUKEE, WISCONSIN

While eggs lend frothiness to a recipe, there is a slight risk associated with eating raw eggs. To minimize the risk, use pasteurized eggs.

Dividing egg whites can be tricky. One egg white is equal to approximately 2 tablespoons. The tablespoon needed for this recipe will be much easier to measure after the egg whites have been beaten slightly to make them more liquid. Easier yet, just double the recipe and sip with a friend!

KRINGLE SYRUP MAKES ABOUT 2½ CUPS

1 cup unsalted, halved raw walnuts

1 cup dried cranberries

1 cup julienned peeled fresh ginger

2 cups granulated sugar

2 cups water

➤ Preheat the oven to 350 degrees F. Spread the walnuts evenly on a cookie sheet and bake until they are aromatic and begin to brown, 8 to 10 minutes. Remove from the oven.

➤ Combine the toasted walnuts with the cranberries, ginger, sugar, and water in a medium saucepan and bring to a simmer over medium-low heat. Simmer for 20 minutes, stirring occasionally. Remove from the heat and let the ingredients steep while cooling. Once cooled, strain through a coffee filter into a clean glass container. Cover and refrigerate for up to 2 weeks.

RITTENHOUSE INN WASSAIL PUNCH

SERVES
★
10 TO 12

TOOLS

CHEESECLOTH
KITCHEN
STRING
LARGE POT

GLASSES

MUGS

GARNISH

GROUND
NUTMEG
1 CINNAMON
STICK
PER DRINK

Wassail is a deeply rooted tradition in the Midwest and a popular regional staple throughout the cold-weather season. Every winter as the holidays approach, many Wisconsinites still take part in the age-old "wassailing of apple trees," a ritual dating back to the fifteenth century that involves sprinkling wassail on apple trees to ensure a strong, healthy harvest and to keep the trees safe from evil spirits. Wassail always blends apples and winter holiday spices, but the sweeteners and spirits often vary from recipe to recipe. This version comes from the Rittenhouse Inn in Bayfield, an area that leads apple production in Wisconsin. The cranberry juice is a perfectly tart counterpart to the sweetness of the apple cider and brown sugar; the bourbon lends a full, rich quality; and the ginger, pepper, and spices offer a final kick of flavor.

WASSAIL:

12 whole cloves

6 whole allspice berries

½ inch fresh ginger root, peeled and sliced

3 cinnamon sticks

12 whole white peppercorns

1 gallon fresh apple cider

6 ounces cranberry juice

¾ cup packed light brown sugar

10 to 12 ounces bourbon

➤ To make the wassail, wrap the cloves, allspice, ginger, cinnamon sticks, and peppercorns in cheesecloth and tie with kitchen string. Combine the cider, cranberry juice, brown sugar, and spice bag in a large pot over high heat. Bring to a boil, then reduce the heat and simmer for 30 minutes.

➤ For each serving, put one ounce of the bourbon in a mug and fill with hot Wassail. Garnish with a dusting of nutmeg and a cinnamon stick.

JULIE PHILLIPS
RITTENHOUSE INN, BAYFIELD, WISCONSIN

A.C.003
TIP

The Wassail can be stored for several days in a covered container in the refrigerator. If you like lots of spice, you can make it a day ahead and leave the spice bag in the container overnight.

TOM AND JERRY

While the rest of the country celebrates the holidays with thick, creamy eggnog, Midwesterners keep a different tradition alive: warm and frothy Tom and Jerrys. Though the drink's origin is still a matter of debate, it hails from the 1800s and is made by mixing a whipped, eggy batter with warmed spirits and either hot water or milk. It was wildly popular for decades until Prohibition knocked it off the mixological radar. It made a spirited comeback in the 1950s as the life of the era's Tom and Jerry parties but soon fell out of fashion again—except in the Midwest, where it's still the winter warmer of choice. Every frigid winter, the region's supermarkets stock up on tubs of the batter, but bartenders and cocktail consultants Ira Koplowitz and Nicholas Kosevich prefer to make theirs from scratch, putting an updated spin on the old-school classic. "Nearly every recipe calls for equal parts egg whites and yolks, but we found it a more enjoyable cocktail with less yolk." They also use bourbon instead of rum, to better balance the drink's sweetness.

SERVES

★

4

TOOLS

ELECTRIC MIXER WITH WHISK ATTACHMENT

TIN COCKTAIL SHAKER

HEAT-RESISTANT BOWL

BARSPOON

GLASSES

GLASS MUGS

GARNISH

GROUND CINNAMON

BATTER:

2 eggs

1 ounce Paul Masson brandy

¼ cup granulated sugar

¼ teaspoon ground allspice

¼ teaspoon ground cinnamon

⅛ teaspoon ground cloves

½ teaspoon vanilla extract

3 ounces bourbon

3 ounces Paul Masson brandy

2 ounces Simple Syrup (page 33)

12 ounces whole milk, warmed

To make the batter, separate the eggs, setting aside one of the yolks for another use (see Tip, page 72). With an electric mixer fitted with the whisk attachment, beat the egg whites until stiff peaks form; set aside. In a small bowl, whisk the egg yolk, brandy, sugar, allspice, cinnamon, cloves, and vanilla until the mixture lightens in color and thickens, about 8 minutes. Gently fold the egg whites into the yolk mixture, one-quarter at a time, being careful not to deflate the whites.

For each serving, put 2 heaping tablespoons of the batter in a heated glass mug. Combine ¾ ounce of the bourbon, ¾ ounce of the brandy, and ½ ounce of the simple syrup in a metal cocktail shaker, then place the shaker in a bowl of hot water. After 30 seconds, pour the warmed spirits over the batter in the mug and top with 3 ounces of the milk. The batter will sit at the top of the mugs. Stir beneath the batter to incorporate the milk, syrup, and spirits. Garnish with a dusting of cinnamon.

IRA KOPLOWITZ AND NICHOLAS KOSEVICH
BITTERCUBE, MILWAUKEE, WISCONSIN

THE URBAN PRAIRIE

While it might not technically be part of America's Great Plains, Illinois is nonetheless a state blanketed in prairie land, and Chicago bartender Charles Joly created this cocktail as an homage to his home state's rustic beauty. The recipe features gin from North Shore, which is a small-batch distillery in Lake Bluff, Illinois, along with a bitter ale from Chicago craft brewer Half Acre. The result is an incredibly nuanced cocktail that's anything but plain.

SERVES
★
1

TOOLS

COCKTAIL
SHAKER
FINE-MESH
STRAINER
BARSPOON

GLASS

COLLINS

GARNISH

2 OR 3 PIECES
OF TALL
PRAIRIE GRASS
TIED TOGETHER

¾ ounce peach purée (see Note)

1 ounce Fresh Sour Mix (facing page)

1¼ ounces North Shore No. 6 gin

¾ ounce Grand Marnier

Ice cubes, for shaking

Cracked ice, for serving

1½ ounces Half Acre Over Ale (see Tip)

→ Combine the peach purée, sour mix, gin, and Grand Marnier in a cocktail shaker, add the ice cubes, and shake well. Strain into a Collins glass filled with cracked ice. Top with the ale, stir to combine, and garnish with the prairie grass.

**CHARLES JOLY
THE DRAWING ROOM, CHICAGO, ILLINOIS**

NOTE To make the peach purée, peel and pit 1 fresh, ripe peach and purée in a food processor with a squeeze of fresh lemon juice. Strain through a fine-mesh strainer and add Simple Syrup (page 33) to taste.

If you don't want to make the peach purée from scratch, you can purchase a delicious bottled version online from the Perfect Purée of Napa Valley (see Resources, page 121).

TIP If you can't find Half Acre Over Ale in your area, look for a medium-bodied beer with a nice balance of malt flavor and hoppy bitterness.

FRESH SOUR MIX MAKES 1½ CUPS

| 1 cup fresh lemon juice | ½ cup Simple Syrup (page 33) |

➤ Combine the lemon juice and simple syrup in a clean glass container. Stir until blended. Cover and refrigerate for up to 2 weeks.

CHAPTER ★ FOUR

A.C. **004** A.C.

In the arid, dusty desert, a mirage plays tricks on the eye, conjuring up a watery oasis on the otherwise dry desert floor. But beyond the shimmery images, tumbleweeds, and ghost towns of John Wayne's Wild West, THE AMERICAN WEST FLOWS RICH WITH CULTURE, HISTORY, AND FLAVORS UNLIKE THOSE FOUND ANYWHERE ELSE IN THE COUNTRY. This is a multicolored land of cactus-filled deserts, river-carved canyons, and fresh mountain air that serves as a natural backdrop for contemporary cocktails full of regional flair. Bartenders from the Grand Canyon to the Gulf Coast are pairing local spirits with native fruits, herbs, and even cactus in drinks that are as full of color and flavor as the desert scenery itself. A reflection of the region's diverse cultures and landscape, these tangible thirst-quenchers offer up the real flavors of the American West.

AGAVE WAY

As the unofficial chile capital of the United States, New Mexico leads the country's chile pepper production. With more than a dozen cultivars thriving in the state's dry desert soil, it's no surprise that Santa Fe barman Chris Milligan would infuse cocktails with chiles' piquant punch. Think you can't take the heat? Don't worry—the sweet and smooth flavors of another desert plant, the agave, balance the slight heat for a cocktail that is light and refreshing. If you have trouble finding chile peppers specifically labeled as a "New Mexico" variety, you can substitute an Anaheim pepper, which belongs to the same family.

SERVES
★
1

TOOLS

MUDDLER
COCKTAIL
SHAKER
FINE-MESH
STRAINER

GLASS

COCKTAIL

GARNISH

GRAPE
CHILE RING

½-inch-thick ring of fresh New Mexico green chile, seeded

5 black or red grapes

½ ounce fresh lime juice

½ ounce dark agave syrup, diluted (see Tip)

2 ounces reposado tequila

Ice cubes

 Muddle the chile ring, grapes, lime juice, and agave syrup in a cocktail shaker. Add the tequila and shake well with ice. Strain into a chilled cocktail glass and garnish with a skewered grape and chile ring.

CHRIS MILLIGAN
SECRETO LOUNGE, SANTA FE, NEW MEXICO

A.C.004 TIP Agave syrup, also called agave nectar, is made with the juice from the heart of the desert-dwelling agave plant. After extraction, the liquid is then heated and reduced into a syrup that is slightly less thick than honey, but sweeter. The color and flavor are determined by the amount of heat used, with darker syrups offering richer, more caramel-like flavors. In this cocktail, Milligan dilutes dark agave syrup to keep the cocktail from becoming overly sweet, stirring one part hot water into three parts syrup and letting it come to room temperature before using.

DESERT TRIO

It's often said that good things come in threes, and this cocktail from veteran Las Vegas bartender Sean Bigley is proof. Using three plants that thrive in the desert of Nevada—agave, aloe vera, and sage—Bigley's cocktail is the perfect respite from the arid heat. The roasted-agave tequila finds a soothing synergy with the fresh aloe, while the green Chartreuse highlights the herby characteristics of the sage. And true to the glitz and glam of Vegas, he tops it all off with a sprinkling of edible silver, an all-too-apropos finish for a cocktail hailing from the Silver State.

SERVES
★
1

TOOLS

MUDDLER
COCKTAIL
SHAKER
FINE-MESH
STRAINER

GLASS

COCKTAIL

GARNISH

EDIBLE SILVER
FLAKES
(OPTIONAL)
1 SAGE LEAF

4 whole sage leaves	1½ ounces El Sol aloe vera juice (see Tip)
½ ounce fresh lime juice	½ ounce green Chartreuse
1½ ounces reposado tequila	Ice cubes

Muddle the sage leaves and lime juice in a cocktail shaker. Add the tequila, aloe vera juice, and Chartreuse and shake well with ice. Double strain into a chilled cocktail glass. Sprinkle a bit of edible silver flakes, if desired, onto a sage leaf and float on top of the cocktail.

SEAN BIGLEY
FONTANA BAR, BELLAGIO, LAS VEGAS, NEVADA

A.C.004
TIP

Aloe isn't just for slathering on sunburned skin. The mildly flavored juice adds a slight earthy element to cocktails. Commercial brands such as El Sol offer bottled versions that can be found in the refrigerated juice section at natural grocers.

DR. SCOLA

Back in 1885, a Texan by the name of Charles Alderton invented a distinctively flavored soda called Dr Pepper. Today that soda is sold all over the world and has become an American classic, but there's only one place still producing the original formula, and that's in the tiny town of Dublin, Texas. Texans are fiercely proud of their state's iconic Dr Pepper, and every year some sixty thousand visitors flock to Dublin to see the bottling plant firsthand (there's a museum and on-site tours) and to stock up on as much of the soda as they can carry away. This cocktail from Houston bartender Robert Heugel is a tribute to the original Dr Pepper and to Rockets player Luis Scola, another pride of Texas, whose Argentinean roots take him to Heugel's bar, Anvil, for the occasional Fernet and Coke. One night, after a visit from Scola, Heugel decided to combine the Fernet with rum, bitters, and a splash of Dublin Dr Pepper, and the Dr. Scola was born. Charles Alderton would be proud indeed.

SERVES

1

TOOLS

MUDDLER
BARSPOON

GLASS

DOUBLE
OLD FASHIONED

GARNISH

BRANDIED
CHERRIES
(PAGE 27)

---

1 small circular slice of orange zest

2 dashes of Fee Brothers Old Fashion aromatic bitters

1 ounce white rum

1 ounce Fernet-Branca

Ice cubes

3 to 4 ounces Original Dublin Dr Pepper

Muddle the orange zest with the bitters in a double Old Fashioned glass. Add the rum, Fernet-Branca, and ice and stir until chilled. Top with the Dr Pepper and garnish with a brandied cherry or two, skewered on a cocktail pick.

ROBERT HEUGEL
ANVIL, HOUSTON, TEXAS

HOTEL 43

"It's those Idaho potatoes, you know," quips Pat Carden, bar manager at Chandlers restaurant in Boise, referring to the smoothness of Idaho's own Blue Ice vodka. Crafted solely from the Russet Burbank potatoes that Idaho is so famous for, Blue Ice is distilled in a four-column still and then filtered five times. Carden mixes the assertive yet silky spirit with a liqueur made from Idaho's official state fruit, the huckleberry, foraged from the local wilderness, for his Hotel 43 cocktail. The name refers to the hotel that houses Chandlers, as well as the state's connection to the number 43—not only was Idaho the 43rd state admitted to the Union, but Boise happens to sit on the 43rd parallel.

SERVES

1

TOOLS

MIXING GLASS
BARSPOON
FINE-MESH
STRAINER

GLASS

COCKTAIL

GARNISH

LEMON TWIST

2 ounces Blue Ice vodka

¾ ounce citrus vodka

½ ounce H huckleberry liqueur

¼ ounce fresh lemon juice

Ice cubes

➤ Combine the vodkas, liqueur, and lemon juice in a mixing glass, add ice, and stir until chilled. Strain into a chilled cocktail glass and garnish with the lemon twist.

PAT CARDEN
CHANDLERS, HOTEL 43, BOISE, IDAHO

LOQUACIOUS

Texans claim that everything is bigger in the Longhorn State, and David Alan, keeper of the blog Tipsy Texan, lives up to that philosophy by going big on local ingredients in this flavorful cocktail. Locals know that come spring, loquats are ripe for the picking. This evergreen shrub, with fruit flavors somewhat akin to an apricot, grows prolifically in Alan's Austin neighborhood. He mixes a handful of them with Tito's vodka, which is crafted in Texas's first and oldest legal distillery, and Paula's Texas Lemon, an Italian-style limoncello liqueur with just the right amount of mouth-puckering tartness. The final product boasts bold, beautiful flavors as grandiose as the state's great claims.

SERVES
★
1

TOOLS

MUDDLER
COCKTAIL
SHAKER
FINE-MESH
STRAINER

GLASS

COCKTAIL

GARNISH

MINT SPRIG

6 ripe loquats, quartered and seeded (see Tip)

½ ounce Simple Syrup (page 33)

1½ ounces Tito's Handmade vodka

½ ounce Paula's Texas lemon liqueur or other limoncello

½ ounce fresh lime juice

Ice cubes

→ Muddle the loquats and simple syrup in a cocktail shaker. Add the vodka, liqueur, and lime juice and shake vigorously with ice. Double strain into a chilled cocktail glass and garnish with the mint sprig.

DAVID ALAN
TIPSY TEXAN BLOG, AUSTIN, TEXAS

If you can't find loquats, Alan suggests substituting quartered, pitted apricots, which are similar in flavor.

RATTLESNAKE

There is still plenty of wild left in the West. Hidden off the trails, deep in the shadows of the Rocky Mountains, rattlesnakes thrive, but a snake of a different breed has found its way into Colorado's cocktail culture: the classic quaff from Harry Craddock's *The Savoy Cocktail Book*. Reimagined by Boulder barman Evan Faber, this robust sipper invites two Colorado distillates into the mix, Stranahan's whiskey and Leopold Bros. absinthe. Stranahan's is a small-batch whiskey crafted from local barley and fresh mountain springwater, and the absinthe is a blend of anise, sweet fennel, and grand wormwood. Together they seamlessly combine with fresh citrus and egg whites into a sophisticated drink that's surprisingly tame in light of its venomous name.

SERVES
★
1

TOOLS

COCKTAIL
SHAKER
FINE-MESH
STRAINER

GLASS

COCKTAIL

GARNISH

LEMON TWIST

3 drops of Leopold Bros. absinthe verte

Ice cubes

1½ ounces Stranahan's Colorado whiskey

¾ ounce fresh lemon juice

½ ounce Simple Syrup (page 33)

1 fresh egg white (see Tip, page 72)

Add the absinthe to an ice-filled cocktail shaker and shake about four times. Add the whiskey, lemon juice, simple syrup, and egg white and shake vigorously. Double strain into a chilled cocktail glass and garnish with the lemon twist.

EVAN FABER
SALT, BOULDER, COLORADO

PRICKLY RICKY

Commonly found throughout the dusty desert landscapes of the Southwest, prickly pear is a member of the cactus family, and its plump, earthy fruit has been a popular part of Native American diets for centuries. This spiny-skinned fruit, which is also called a cactus fig, is a staple of Southwestern cuisine, making its way into everything from condiments to cocktails. "Prickly pear syrup is a great addition to any cocktail," says Robert Byrd, bartender at the James Beard–nominated St. Francis restaurant in Phoenix, "because it offers a complexity of flavors that are at the same time sweet and refreshing."

SERVES
★
1

TOOLS

BARSPOON

GLASS

COLLINS

GARNISH

LEMON TWIST

1 ounce blanco tequila

1 ounce Prickly Pear Syrup (facing page; see Tip)

1 ounce fresh lemon juice

2 ounces light lager

Ice cubes

➤ Add the tequila, prickly pear syrup, lemon juice, and lager one at a time into an ice-filled Collins glass. Gently stir, then garnish with the lemon twist.

ROBERT BYRD
ST. FRANCIS, PHOENIX, ARIZONA

PRICKLY PEAR SYRUP MAKES ABOUT 3 CUPS

12 fresh prickly pears, burrs removed with tongs and skin intact

1½ tablespoons fresh lemon juice

0.44 oz. powdered fruit pectin (a quarter of a 1¾ oz. packet)

3 cups granulated sugar

Process the pears in an electric juicer. You should have about 2 cups of juice. Combine the prickly pear juice, lemon juice, and pectin in a large saucepan over high heat and bring to a boil. Add the sugar and return mixture to a boil. Cook for 1 minute without stirring and then remove from the heat. Cool to room temperature and stir before transferring to a clean glass container. Cover and refrigerate for up to 2 weeks.

JEAN GROEN
BOYCE THOMPSON ARBORETUM, SUPERIOR, ARIZONA

While some desert dwellers use prickly pears to make a syrup at home, online purveyors, such as Cheri's Desert Harvest (see Resources, page 119), sell premade prickly pear syrup.

VERDE MARIA

Sometimes it's hard to believe that anything can grow in the water-deprived desert climate of Arizona, but some plants, such as the paper-husked tomatillo, actually thrive in the heat-drenched environment. And thanks to its earthy, lemony tang, this Latin American culinary staple also harmonizes deliciously in mixed drinks, like this one from Flagstaff bartender Katie Dembs. The small mountain town of Flagstaff, known as the gateway to the Grand Canyon, sees nearly five million visitors each year, and the Criollo Latin Kitchen, just off of the historic Route 66, is always ready for the masses with a batch of its housemade salsa verde. Playing off of those traditional saucy flavors, Dembs combines fresh tomatillos with red onion, cilantro, avocado, and añejo tequila for a savory sipper that could be considered its own gateway to the culinary crossover of the tomatillo.

SERVES
★
1

TOOLS

BLENDER
BARSPOON

GLASS

COLLINS

GARNISH

LIME WHEEL
CILANTRO
SPRIG

---

2 ounces añejo tequila

2 tomatillos, peeled and sliced

½ teaspoon chopped red onion

6 fresh cilantro leaves

¼ ripe avocado

¾-inch ring of fresh jalapeño chile, seeded

½ ounce fresh lime juice

Ice cubes

2 ounces lager

Combine the tequila, tomatillos, onion, cilantro leaves, avocado, chile ring, and lime juice in a blender and blend on the highest setting until smooth, about 20 seconds. Pour into an ice-filled Collins glass, top with the lager, and stir gently. Garnish with the lime wheel and cilantro sprig.

KATIE DEMBS
CRIOLLO LATIN KITCHEN, FLAGSTAFF, ARIZONA

ROCKY MOUNTAIN HANDSHAKE

SERVES
★
6

TOOLS

MIXING GLASS
BARSPOON
FINE-MESH
STRAINER

GLASSES

DOUBLE ROCKS

The Mile-High City is an out-and-out mecca for beer, with seventy-four breweries residing in the greater Denver area. But home to more than just breweries, Denver hosts the Great American Beer Festival, an annual suds-soaked event that draws an international craft beer–loving crowd. In homage to this frothy beer culture, barman Kevin Burke created what he calls the Rocky Mountain Handshake by mixing beer and whiskey from two of Colorado's favorite artisans, Avery Brewing Co. and Leopold Bros. distillery. Avery's The Reverend is a dry, quadruple ale that tops out at 10 percent ABV, so adding Leopold Bros.' open-barrel fermented whiskey "could be considered somewhat gilding the lily," according to Burke. Still, the two blend beautifully when mixed with Demerara syrup and Ramazzotti, a bittersweet amaro. And true to its welcoming name, this cocktail is made to serve a small crowd, so be sure to gather some friends before mixing.

4 ounces Leopold Bros. small-batch whiskey

¾ ounce Ramazzotti

¾ ounce Demerara Syrup (page 70)

Ice cubes

21 ounces Avery's The Reverend ale

→ Combine the whiskey, Ramazzotti, and Demerara syrup in a mixing glass, add ice, and stir until chilled. Strain equally into six double rocks glasses (about 1 ounce in each glass). Top each glass with 3½ ounces of the chilled ale. Stir gently to combine.

KEVIN BURKE
COLT & GRAY, DENVER, COLORADO

CHAPTER ★ FIVE

WEST COAST

A.C. **005** A.C.

The West Coast may be known more for its stubborn individuality than its long-standing cocktail traditions. Here, it's more about attitude than protocol. INGENUITY, RESOURCEFULNESS, AND FREEWHEELING CREATIVITY ARE THE ORDER OF THE DAY, and that spirit, combined with the exceptional produce that flourishes in the West Coast's fertile soils and temperate climate, brings a certain freshness and flair to the region's shakers. Bartenders find inspiration in the teeming farmers' markets and rolling vineyards. And they use the bounty of fresh fruits, vegetables, and herbs to craft their own housemade cocktail ingredients, such as bitters, infusions, and tinctures. Without a generations-old cocktail culture of its own, the West Coast is a place where bartenders are free to experiment and push boundaries, drawing inspiration from the area's multicultural population and putting a personal spin on the classics. From the Asian-influenced tropics of Hawaii to the rain-soaked streets of the Pacific Northwest, cocktails on the West Coast are clearly a spirited bunch.

BRIAR PATCH

Blackberries, marionberries, raspberries—brambly berry bushes thrive all over the Pacific Northwest. While many locals enjoy their berries fresh in everything from pies to pancakes, they also stock their pantries with berry jams and jellies for year-round use. This recipe, from Portland bartender Jeffrey Morgenthaler, incorporates marionberry jam to play off a classic Bramble cocktail by London bartender Dick Bradsell. The earthy, complex marionberry, created in the 1940s at Oregon State University when a researcher crossbred two lesser-known blackberry varieties, has become one of the most popular cultivated berries in Oregon. The marionberry jam used in this cocktail complements the raspberry notes in the Small's gin, from Oregon's own Ransom Spirits, while the fresh citrus adds a welcome acidity to the finished drink.

SERVES
★
1

TOOLS

COCKTAIL SHAKER
FINE-MESH STRAINER

GLASS

OLD FASHIONED

GARNISH

3 FRESH MARIONBERRIES
××OR××
BLACKBERRIES
××OR××
RASPBERRIES

(OPTIONAL)

½ ounce Rich Simple Syrup (page 100; see Tip)

1½ ounces Small's gin

¾ ounce fresh lemon juice

1 teaspoon marionberry jam

Ice cubes, for shaking

Crushed ice, for serving

Combine the simple syrup, gin, lemon juice, and marionberry jam in a cocktail shaker, add ice cubes, and shake well. Double strain into an Old Fashioned glass filled with crushed ice. Garnish with the berries, if desired, skewered on a cocktail pick.

JEFFREY MORGENTHALER
CLYDE COMMON, PORTLAND, OREGON

Since the jam in this recipe is also sweet, feel free to adjust the amount of simple syrup you use in the cocktail, depending on how sweet you like your drinks.

RICH SIMPLE SYRUP MAKES ABOUT 2 CUPS

| 1 cup water | 2 cups sugar |

→ Combine the water and sugar in a small saucepan and bring to a boil. Reduce the heat to medium-low and simmer, stirring slowly until the sugar is dissolved, 2 to 3 minutes. Remove from the heat and let cool to room temperature. Transfer to a clean glass container, cover, and refrigerate for up to 2 weeks.

1022 MARTINI

Douglas fir trees thrive throughout the forests of Oregon and Washington, and every year, Oregon distiller Stephen McCarthy picks the springtime buds of these trees by hand and infuses them into a distinctly Northwestern eau de vie. Looking for a way to showcase this brandy, Tacoma bartender Chris Keil created this cocktail, combining the delicate woodsy flavor of the eau de vie with the layered botanicals of gin and Lillet to delicious effect. It's truly a taste of the Pacific Northwest.

SERVES
★
1

TOOLS

MIXING GLASS
BARSPOON
FINE-MESH
STRAINER

GLASS

COCKTAIL

2 ounces gin

½ ounce Lillet blanc

½ ounce Clear Creek Douglas fir eau de vie

Ice cubes

→ Combine the gin, Lillet blanc, and eau de vie in a mixing glass, add ice, and stir until chilled. Strain into a chilled cocktail glass.

CHRIS KEIL
1022 SOUTH, TACOMA, WASHINGTON

EL COLIBRÍ

With numerous apiaries dotting the Bay Area and urban beekeeping bigger than ever, San Francisco is buzzing over locally harvested honey. And the natural sweetener is creating a splash in cocktails as well, thanks in part to Mission district bartender Vince Lund, who uses a local honey syrup in his El Colibrí cocktail. Translating to "hummingbird" in Spanish, the El Colibrí balances robust reposado tequila, sweet black currant liqueur, and rich honey syrup with a slight lemon tartness on the finish. For this cocktail, Lund recommends using a raw, organic honey, like the mildly floral-flavored orange blossom variety, to fully play off the smoky notes of the roasted agave in the reposado tequila.

SERVES
★
1

TOOLS

COCKTAIL
SHAKER
FINE-MESH
STRAINER

GLASS

COUPE

GARNISH

1-INCH-BY-
2-INCH PIECE
OF LEMON PEEL

¾ ounce honey syrup (see Note)

2 ounces reposado tequila

1½ ounces fresh lemon juice

½ ounce crème de cassis

Ice cubes

→ Combine the honey syrup, tequila, lemon juice, and crème de cassis in a cocktail shaker with ice. Shake vigorously so the honey creates a nice head on the cocktail. Double strain into a chilled coupe and garnish with the lemon peel.

VINCE LUND
BERETTA, SAN FRANCISCO, CALIFORNIA

A.C.005
NOTE

To make honey syrup, mix 2 parts honey with 1 part warm water. Stir well and let cool.

EVA PERÓN

You won't find many cities with as strong an affinity for Fernet-Branca as San Francisco. Like the generations of Italian Americans who call the city home, locals sip the bitter and bold Italian amaro, which is a staple ingredient in cocktails found across San Francisco, straight as a digestif or followed by a chaser of ginger ale. Created by Darren Crawford of Bourbon & Branch, this recipe (whose name is inspired by another Fernet-loving culture: Argentina) combines that classic combo of Fernet and ginger for a potent cocktail that proves bitter can in fact be bella.

SERVES
★
1

TOOLS

COCKTAIL
SHAKER
FINE-MESH
STRAINER

GLASS

COLLINS

GARNISH

LIME WHEEL

1 ounce Fernet-Branca

1 ounce Carpano Antica sweet vermouth

1 ounce Domaine de Canton ginger liqueur

1 ounce fresh lime juice

Ice cubes

1 ounce ginger beer

➤ Combine the Fernet-Branca, vermouth, ginger liqueur, and lime juice in an ice-filled cocktail shaker. Shake well and strain into an ice-filled Collins glass. Top with the ginger beer and garnish with the lime wheel.

DARREN CRAWFORD
BOURBON & BRANCH, SAN FRANCISCO, CALIFORNIA

MISS PETTIGROVE

Oregon is home to some of the world's best-tasting hazelnuts (also known as filberts), and farms throughout the state cultivate these rich, flavor-packed nuts. This recipe from award-winning Portland bartender Suzanne Allard makes a delicious after-dinner cocktail and provides a decadent taste of the Northwest, with a combination of locally made chocolate vodka, locally grown hazelnuts, and Belle de Brillet, a nod to the area's abundance of pear orchards.

SERVES
★
1

TOOLS

MIXING GLASS
BARSPOON
FINE-MESH
STRAINER

GLASS

COCKTAIL

¾ ounce Belle de Brillet pear liqueur

Salty toasted hazelnuts (see Note)

1¼ ounces Mud Puddle chocolate vodka (see Tip)

2 dashes of Angostura bitters

Ice cubes

Wet the rim of a cocktail glass with some of the pear liqueur, then dip the glass into the salty toasted hazelnuts to coat the rim. Set aside. Combine the vodka, pear liqueur, and bitters in a mixing glass, add ice, and stir until chilled. Strain carefully into the rimmed cocktail glass.

SUZANNE ALLARD
GILT CLUB, PORTLAND, OREGON

NOTE To make salty toasted hazelnuts, preheat the broiler, spread ¼ cup of raw hazelnuts evenly on a cookie sheet, and place under the broiler for about 5 minutes; let cool. In a food processor, pulse the toasted nuts until finely ground. In a shallow dish, mix 2 parts ground nuts with 1 part kosher salt.

TIP If you can't find New Deal's Mud Puddle chocolate vodka, you can substitute another brand, such as Van Gogh.

MURASAKI GEISHA

With a significant Japanese influence on both culture and cuisine, saké is one of the most widely enjoyed drinks on the islands of Hawaii, and at Doraku Sushi in Honolulu, you can find an array of sakés from around the world. One of the best-kept secrets about saké is that it's equally as good in cocktails as it is sipped solo. Nigori, which is an unfiltered saké, makes an especially delicious addition to cocktails with its sweet, creamy backbone. For this recipe, bartender Ikaika Villa combines nigori with the botanicals of gin and a tart-sweet raspberry liqueur for a luscious taste of the islands.

SERVES
★
1

TOOLS

MUDDLER
COCKTAIL
SHAKER
FINE-MESH
STRAINER

GLASS

FLUTE

GARNISH

3 FRESH
RASPBERRIES
××OR××
BLACKBERRIES

1½ ounces Chambord raspberry liqueur

3 to 4 fresh raspberries or blackberries

Ice cubes

1 ounce nigori saké (see Tip)

½ ounce gin

 Muddle the raspberry liqueur and berries in a cocktail shaker. Shake with ice and strain into a flute. Discard the ice, rinse the shaker, and add the saké, gin, and more ice and shake vigorously. Strain over the liqueur mixture, pouring gently to create a layered effect. Garnish with the berries.

IKAIKA VILLA
DORAKU SUSHI, HONOLULU, HAWAII

A.C.005 TIP Be sure to use a premium nigori for this cocktail, as the quality will make a difference in the flavor. If you have leftover saké, you can store it in the refrigerator for up to 2 weeks.

NORTH BY NORTHWEST

West Coast chefs and bartenders are known for their love of local, seasonal food and drink, and at Laurelhurst Market in Portland, Oregon, bartender Evan Zimmerman abides by this garden-to-glass ethos for his cocktails. True to its name, this recipe showcases ingredients from the Pacific Northwest, home to some of the country's most popular apple varieties, including Golden Delicious, which are grown on the northeast slope of Mt. Hood and make their way into Oregon's Clear Creek apple brandy. In this cocktail, the smooth, flavorful brandy marries deliciously with the tartness of lemon and apple juice, while the Averna, a bitter Italian amaro, provides boldness and the apple butter lends a velvety texture. When apple season hits every fall, this recipe is a lovely reminder to take full advantage of that bounty.

SERVES
★
1

TOOLS

COCKTAIL SHAKER
FINE-MESH STRAINER

GLASS

COCKTAIL

1½ ounces Clear Creek apple brandy

¾ ounce fresh lemon juice

¾ ounce fresh-pressed apple juice

½ ounce Averna

1 teaspoon apple butter (see Tip)

Ice cubes

➤ Combine the brandy, lemon juice, apple juice, Averna, and apple butter in an ice-filled cocktail shaker. Shake well and double strain into a chilled cocktail glass.

EVAN ZIMMERMAN
LAURELHURST MARKET, PORTLAND, OREGON

There's no butter in apple butter. It's basically a thicker form of applesauce that's made by cooking apples down slowly with apple cider until they caramelize and turn the "butter" brown.

PERSIMMON MARGARITA

Los Angeles is famous for its year-round farmers' markets, and at the Hungry Cat in Hollywood, fresh, seasonal ingredients play a starring role on the cocktail menu. This unique recipe is a nod to Southern California's abundance of persimmons as well as the area's affinity for tequila. "Persimmons are always great around November and December, and at their best, they have a warm, spicelike flavor that complements tequila and lime," says bartender Tim Staehling. "Since winters in Los Angeles are mostly warm and sunny, this is a summer drink with a winter twist."

SERVES
★
1

TOOLS

COCKTAIL SHAKER
FINE-MESH STRAINER

GLASS

COCKTAIL

GARNISH

LIME WHEEL

Lime wedge
Cinnamon-salt (see Note)
1½ ounces persimmon purée (see Note)

1¾ ounces reposado tequila
1 ounce fresh lime juice
Ice cubes

→ Wet the rim of a cocktail glass with the lime wedge and dip it in the cinnamon-salt. Set aside. Combine the persimmon purée, tequila, and lime juice in a cocktail shaker with ice. Shake vigorously and strain carefully into the rimmed cocktail glass. Garnish with the lime wheel.

TIM STAEHLING
THE HUNGRY CAT, LOS ANGELES, CALIFORNIA

To make the cinnamon-salt, mix equal parts cinnamon and salt in a shallow dish.

To make the persimmon purée, in a blender or juicer, purée 2 or 3 persimmons (skin and all), adding ½ ounce of Simple Syrup (see page 33) or to taste.

Persimmons are divided into two categories, astringent and nonastringent. Fuyus are the most commonly available nonastringent variety, and they lose their tannic quality sooner than their astringent counterparts, making them easier to use in cocktails.

STRAWBERRY FIELDS

When you think of California wines, Napa immediately comes to mind, but the state is home to dozens of similarly stellar wine regions. Consider this: Of the 165 American Viticultural Areas in the United States, California has the overwhelming majority with 93. While wine gets the lion's share of attention, the state is just as famous for its jewel-like produce, and these two elements come together deliciously in this elegant drink from the award-winning Cyrus Restaurant in Sonoma County. Inspired by the bounty around her, bartender Erika Frey created a drink that blends floral, herbal, and fruity notes into a light and lovely springtime cocktail using local ingredients. For a touch of luxury, she tops it all off with a sparkling wine foam.

SERVES
★
1

TOOLS

MUDDLER
COCKTAIL
SHAKER
FINE-MESH
STRAINER

GLASS

COCKTAIL

GARNISH

SPARKLING
WINE FOAM
(FACING PAGE)
STRAWBERRY
POWDER
(SEE NOTE)

1 fresh strawberry, hulled

Fresh mint sprigs

1 ounce London dry-style gin

½ ounce Dolin Blanc vermouth

¾ ounce dry unoaked white wine, such as Woodenhead French Colombard (see Tip)

¾ ounce fresh lemon juice

½ ounce lavender honey

Ice cubes

Muddle the fresh strawberry and mint sprigs in a cocktail shaker. Add the gin, vermouth, white wine, lemon juice, and lavender honey and shake vigorously with ice. Double strain into a chilled cocktail glass. Top with the wine foam and dust with the strawberry powder.

ERIKA FREY
CYRUS RESTAURANT, HEALDSBURG, CALIFORNIA

To make strawberry powder, pulverize dehydrated strawberries in a spice grinder until powdery.

A sweeter, oaked Chardonnay would overpower this drink with toasty, vanilla flavors and a heavy mouthfeel, so a dry, unoaked Colombard with crisp acidity and floral tones works best.

SPARKLING WINE FOAM MAKES ENOUGH FOAM FOR 2 DRINKS

1 fresh egg white
(see Tip, page 72)

¼ ounce fresh lemon juice

¼ ounce lavender honey

1 ounce sparkling wine (preferably
from Roederer Estate)

With an immersion blender, blend together the egg white, lemon juice,
lavender honey, and sparkling wine. Pour into a rechargeable whipped
cream siphon and charge with nitrous oxide.

STUMPTOWN VANILLA FLIP

The Pacific Northwest is the birthplace of America's specialty coffee culture, and beyond the coffee shops that dot every street corner of the region, bars have gotten in on the action, mixing locally roasted coffee into cocktails like this one from Seattle bartender Andrew Friedman, which features espresso from Stumptown Coffee Roasters. "Their Hair Bender espresso is so expressive that I thought it deserved to be in a cocktail," says Friedman. Taking inspiration from the classic froth of a flip cocktail, this velvety concoction harmonizes the rich, chocolaty notes of the espresso with vanilla-flecked Navan liqueur. Mandarine Napoléon adds the perfect splash of orangey sweetness.

SERVES
★
1

TOOLS

HAWTHORN
STRAINER
2 COCKTAIL
SHAKERS

GLASS

COCKTAIL

GARNISH

ORANGE TWIST

1 fresh egg white
(see Tip, page 72)

2 ounces Navan vanilla liqueur

½ ounce fresh-brewed espresso,
at room temperature

¾ ounce Mandarine Napoléon
orange liqueur

Ice cubes

Put the spring from a Hawthorn strainer and the egg white in a cocktail shaker and shake vigorously until soft peaks form, about 30 seconds; set aside. In a separate cocktail shaker, combine the vanilla liqueur, espresso, and orange liqueur with ice and shake well. Add this mixture to the egg white (with the shaker spring still inside) and quickly shake to combine. Pour into a chilled cocktail glass and garnish with the orange twist.

ANDREW FRIEDMAN
LIBERTY BAR, SEATTLE, WASHINGTON

CALIFORNIA BUBBLE BATH

Faced with the sheer abundance of fresh produce grown year-round in Southern California, Los Angeles–based bartender Matt Biancaniello threw his cocktail menu out the window and decided to let the local farmers' markets guide his offerings. Visiting the markets up to five times a week, Biancaniello stocks his bar with a veritable produce aisle, from arugula to green zebra tomatoes, then sets to work muddling, infusing, and garnishing with his haul. He created this fragrant drink as a testament to the area's Mediterranean climate, where citrus, lavender, and artichokes grow with abandon.

SERVES
★
1

TOOLS

COCKTAIL
SHAKER
FINE-MESH
STRAINER
BARSPOON

GLASS

COLLINS

GARNISH

SMALL SPRIG
OF FRENCH
LAVENDER

2 ounces bourbon

¾ ounce Lavender Syrup
(page 116)

¾ ounce fresh lemon juice

Ice cubes

½ ounce Cynar

→ Combine the bourbon, lavender syrup, and lemon juice in a cocktail shaker, add ice, and shake well. Strain into an ice-filled Collins glass. Float the Cynar on top (see Tip) and garnish with the lavender sprig.

MATT BIANCANIELLO
LIBRARY BAR, THE HOLLYWOOD ROOSEVELT HOTEL, LOS ANGELES, CALIFORNIA

To float the Cynar on top of the drink, hold a barspoon upside down close to the surface of the drink. Carefully pour the liqueur over the back of the barspoon so it gently flows on top of the drink and doesn't penetrate the surface and fall to the bottom. Floating is often done for aesthetic reasons, since it allows bartenders to make eye-catching layers. But it also helps keep a particular ingredient concentrated in flavor rather than dispersed throughout. A sip of this cocktail will offer an immediate hit of Cynar before opening up to the drink's bourbon, lavender, and lemon.

LAVENDER SYRUP MAKES ABOUT 1 CUP

¾ cup water

2 tablespoons dried French
lavender buds

¾ cup granulated sugar

➤ In a small saucepan, bring the water to a boil. Add the lavender buds, remove from the heat, and let steep for 15 minutes. Strain out the lavender and stir the sugar into the lavender water until dissolved, 2 to 3 minutes. Transfer to a clean glass container, cover, and refrigerate for up to 2 weeks.

★ RESOURCES ★

A.C.

Aloe Juice
www.goodkarmabuzz.com

American Classic Rockville Raspberry Tea
www.bigelowtea.com

Angostura Bitters
www.kegworks.com

Blenheim Ginger Ale
www.blenheimshrine.com

Bluecoat Gin
www.bluecoatgin.com

Cheerwine
www.getsomecheerwine.com

Cheri's Desert Harvest
www.cherisdesertharvest.com

Cherry Bitters
www.kegworks.com

Clear Creek Apple Brandy
www.clearcreekdistillery.com

Clear Creek Douglas Fir Eau de Vie
www.clearcreekdistillery.com

Cold River Vodka
www.coldrivervodka.com

Fox's U-Bet Chocolate Syrup
www.foxs-syrups.com

Hank's Root Beer
www.hanksbeverages.net

Heart of the Hudson Apple Vodka
www.tuthilltown.com

Julep Cups
www.thebostonshaker.com

Leopold Bros. Absinthe Verte
www.leopoldbros.com

Leopold Bros. Small-Batch Whiskey
www.leopoldbros.com

L. Mawby Blanc de Noir
www.lmawby.com

Luxardo Marasca Cherries
www.kegworks.com

Maine Wildflower Honey
www.mainebee.com

Michigan Amber Freshwater Rum
www.newhollandbrew.com

Mud Puddle Chocolate Vodka
www.newdealdistillery.com

Paul Masson Brandy
www.paulmassonbrandy.com

Paula's Texas Lemon
www.paulastexaslemon.com

The Perfect Purée of Napa Valley
www.perfectpuree.com

Peychaud's Bitters
www.kegworks.com

Prichards' Crystal Rum
www.prichardsdistillery.com

Red Rock Ginger Ale
www.beveragesdirect.com

Regans' Orange Bitters
www.kegworks.com

Rhubarb Bitters
www.kegworks.com

Stranahan's Colorado Whiskey
www.stranahans.com

Tait Farm Foods
www.taitfarmfoods.com

Templeton Rye Whiskey
www.templetonrye.com

Tito's Handmade Vodka
www.titosvodka.com

Vieux Carré Absinthe
www.vieuxcarreabsinthe.com

Wasmund's Single Malt Whiskey
www.copperfox.biz

Woodchuck Amber Hard Cider
www.woodchuck.com

SOUTH

Belmont Farms
Culpeper, VA
540-825-3207
www.virginiamoonshine.com

Buffalo Trace Distillery
Frankfort, KY
502-696-5926
www.buffalotrace.com

Catoctin Creek Distilling
Purcellville, VA
540-751-8404
www.catoctincreekdistilling.com

Copper Fox Distillery
Sperryville, VA
540-987-8554
www.copperfox.biz

Corsair Artisan Distillery
Bowling Green, KY
615-400-0056
www.corsairartisan.com

Empire Winery & Distillery
New Port Richey, FL
727-819-2821
www.empirewineryanddistillery.com

Fat Dog Spirits
Tampa, FL
813-620-6716
www.fatdogspirits.com

Firefly Distillery
Wadmalaw Island, SC
843-559-6867
www.fireflyvodka.com

Flagler Spirits
Palm Coast, FL
386-986-0641

Four Roses Distillery
Lawrenceburg, KY
502-839-3436
www.fourroses.us

Fugitive Spirits
Nashville, TN
www.fugitivespirits.com

Georgia Distilling Company
Jackson, GA
770-480-6290
www.georgiadistilling.com

Heaven Hill Distilleries
Bardstown, KY
502-348-3921
www.heaven-hill.com

Isaiah Morgan Distillery
Summersville, WV
304-872-7332
www.kirkwood-wine.com

Jim Beam
Clermont, KY
502-543-9877
www.jimbeam.com

Louisville Distilling Co.
Crestwood, KY

Maker's Mark Distillery
Loretto, KY
270-865-2099
www.makersmark.com

MB Roland Distillery
Pembroke, KY
270-640-7744
mbrdistillery.com

Ole Smoky Distillery
Gatlinburg, TN
865-436-6995
olesmokymoonshine.com

Parched Group
Richmond, VA
804-231-3000
www.cirrusvodka.com

Pinchgut Hollow Distillery
Fairmount, WV
304-288-0290
www.pinchguthollowdistillery.com

Prichards' Distillery
Kelso, TN
931-433-5454
www.prichardsdistillery.com

Rock Town Distillery
Little Rock, AR
501-907-5244
www.rocktowndistillery.com

Smooth Ambler Spirits
Maxwelton, WV
304-497-3123
www.smoothambler.com

Southern Artisan Spirits
Kings Mountain, NC
704-297-0191
www.southernartisanspirits.com

Thirteenth Colony Distilleries
Americus, GA
229-924-3310
www.13colony.net

Wild Turkey
Lawrenceburg, KY
502-839-2182
www.wildturkey.com

Woodford Reserve
Versailles, KY
859-879-1812
www.woodfordreserve.com

NORTHEAST

Berkshire Mountain Distillers
Great Barrington, MA
413-429-6280
www.berkshiremountaindistillers.com

Blackwater Distilling
Stevensville, MD
301-758-0936
www.blackwaterdistilling.com

Castle Spirits
Monroe, NY
845-783-8728
www.castlespirits.com

Finger Lakes Distilling
Elmira, NY
607-731-2295
www.fingerlakesdistilling.com

Flag Hill Farm
Vershire, VT
802-685-7724
www.flaghillfarm.com

Green Mountain Distillers
Stowe, VT
802-253-0064
www.greenmountaindistillers.com

Knapp Vineyards
Romulus, NY
800-869-9271
www.knappwine.com

Long Island Spirits
Baiting Hollow, NY
631-630-9322
www.lispirits.com

Maine Distilleries
Freeport, ME
207-865-4828
www.coldrivervodka.com

Mazza Chautauqua Cellars
Mayville, NY
716-269-3000
www.mazzawines.com

Northern Maine Distilling Co.
Houlton, ME
518-505-7243
www.twenty2vodka.com

Philadelphia Distilling
Philadelphia, PA
215-671-0346
www.bluecoatgin.com

Shelburne Orchards Distillery
Shelburne, VT
802-985-2753
www.shelburneorchards.com

Spirits of Maine Distillery
Gouldsboro, ME
207-546-2408
www.bartlettwinery.com

Swedish Hill Vineyard
Romulus, NY
315-549-8326
www.swedishhill.com

Tuthilltown Spirits
Gardiner, NY
845-255-1527
www.tuthilltown.com

Vermont Spirits
St. Johnsbury, VT
802-748-6550
www.vermontspirits.com

Warwick Valley Distillery
Warwick, NY
845-258-4858
www.wvwinery.com

Westford Hill Distillers
Ashford, CT
860-429-0464
www.westfordhill.com

Whistlepig Farm
Shoreham, VT
whistlepigwhiskey.com

Wolf Bros. Distilling
Rochester, NY
585-765-4446

MIDWEST

AEppelTreow Winery & 'Stillery
Burlington, WI
262-878-5345
www.aeppeltreow.com

Amalgamated Distilling Co.
St. Louis, MO
314-771-8500
www.85lashes.com

Cedar Ridge Winery & Distillery
Cedar Rapids, IA
319-362-2778
www.crwine.com

Chateau Chantal Winery & Distillery
Traverse City, MI
231-223-4110
www.chateauchantal.com

Cooper's Chase Distillery
West Point, NE
402-380-0233
www.cooperschase.com

Death's Door Spirits
Door County, WI
608-441-1083
www.deathsdoorspirits.com

Ernest Scarano Distillery
Gibsonburg, OH
419-205-8734
www.esdistillery.com

Great Lakes Distillery
Milwaukee, WI
414-431-8683
www.greatlakesdistillery.com

Heartland Distillers
Indianapolis, IN
800-417-0150
www.heartlanddistillers.com

High Plains Inc.
Atchison, KS
913-773-5780
www.highplainsinc.com

Hubbard's Brandy House
Three Rivers, MI
269-244-5690
www.hubbardsbrandy.com

Koval Distillery
Chicago, IL
312-878-7988
www.koval-distilling.com

McCormick Distilling Co.
Weston, MO
816-640-2276
www.mccormickdistilling.com

Michigan Brewing Company
Webberville, MI
517-521-3600
www.michiganbrewing.com

New Holland Artisan Spirits
Holland, MI
616-355-6422
www.newhollandbrew.com

North Shore Distillery
Lake Bluff, IL
847-574-2499
www.northshoredistillery.com

Solas Distillery
La Vista, NE
402-763-8868
www.jossvodka.com

St. Julian Winery
Paw Paw, MI
269-657-5568
www.stjulian.com

Stonehaven Distilling Co.
Elkhart, IN
574-264-2040

Templeton Rye
Templeton, IA
712-669-8793
www.templetonrye.com

Thatcher's Distillery
Temperance, MI
847-560-3300
www.thatchersorganic.com

Woodstone Creek Distillery
Cincinnati, OH
513-569-0300
www.woodstonecreek.com

Yahara Bay Distillers
Madison, WI
608-692-1858
www.yaharabay.com

WEST

Arizona Distilling Co.
Tempe, AZ
602-391-3889
www.azdistilling.com

Balcones Distilling
Waco, TX
512-294-6735
www.balconesdistilling.com

Bardenay Coeur d'Alene
Coeur d'Alene, ID
208-765-1540
www.bardenay.com

Bardenay Restaurant Distillery
Eagle, ID
208-938-5093
www.bardenay.com

Colorado Gold Distillery
Cedaredge, CO
970-856-2600
www.coloradogolddistillery.com

Colorado Pure Distilling
Denver, CO
303-233-7873
www.coloradopuredistilling.com

Dancing Pines Distillery
Loveland, CO
970-635-3426
www.dpdistillery.com

Don Quixote Distillery
Los Alamos, NM
505-672-3581
www.dqdistillery.com

Downslope Distilling
Centennial, CO
303-693-4300
www.downslopedistilling.com

Fifth Generation Inc.
Austin, TX
512-243-2755
www.titosvodka.com

Graham Barnes Distilling
Austin, TX
512-699-5041
www.treatyoakrum.com

High West Distillery
Park City, UT
435-649-8300
www.highwest.com

Lantrix
Idaho Falls, ID
208-529-8431
www.lantrixliquor.com

Leopold Bros.
Denver, CO
303-307-1515
www.leopoldbros.com

Montanya Distilling Co.
Silverton, CO
970-799-3206
www.montanyadistillers.com

Mystic Mountain Distillery
Larkspur, CO
303-633-9375
www.mysticmtnspirits.com

Ogden's Own Distillery
Odgen, UT
801-458-1995
www.ogdensown.com

Peak Spirits
Hotchkiss, CO
970-835-4916
www.peakspirits.com

Ridge Distillery
Kalispell, MT
406-576-5964
ridgeherbs.com

Rough Stock Distillery
Bozeman, MT
406-579-3986
www.montanawhiskey.com

SAVVY Vodka
Austin, TX
512-476-4477
www.savvyvodka.com

Stranahan's Colorado Whiskey
Denver, CO
303-296-7440
www.stranahans.com

Syntax Spirits
Fort Collins, CO
970-224-1248
www.syntaxspirits.com

WEST COAST

21st Century Spirits
Commerce, CA
323-832-4488
www.21stcenturyspirits.com

Anchor Distilling Co.
San Francisco, CA
415-863-8350
www.anchorbrewing.com

Bainbridge Organic Distillers
Bainbridge Island, WA
206-842-3184
www.bainbridgedistillers.com

Batch 206 Distillery
Seattle, WA
www.batch206.com

Bendistillery
Bend, OR
541-318-0200
www.bendistillery.com

Brandy Peak Distillery
Brookings, OR
541-469-0194
www.brandypeak.com

Bull Run Distillery
Portland, OR
www.bullrundistillery.com

Cascade Peak Spirits
Ashland, OR
541-482-3160
www.organicnationspirits.com

Charbay Winery & Distillery
St. Helena, CA
707-963-9327
www.charbay.com

Clear Creek Distillery
Portland, OR
503-248-9470
www.clearcreekdistillery.com

Deco Distilling
Portland, OR
503-231-7688
www.decodistilling.com

Distillery 209
San Francisco, CA
415-369-0209
www.distillery209.com

Dry Fly Distilling
Spokane, WA
509-489-2112
www.dryflydistilling.com

Eagle Rock Ranch
Redwood Valley, CA
707-468-4661
www.greenwaydistillers.com

Elixir
Eugene, OR
541-345-2257
www.elixir-us.com

Fog's End Distillery
Gonzales, CA
831-809-5941
www.fogsenddistillery.com

Gnostalgic Spirits
Seattle, WA
www.gnostalgicspirits.com

Haleakala Distillers
Kula, HI
808-280-6822
www.haleakaladistillers.com

Hawaiian Islands Spirits
Kahului, HI
808-214-8801
www.paumaui.com

Hood River Distillers
Hood River, OR
541-386-1588
www.hrdspirits.com

House Spirits Distillery
Portland, OR
503-235-3174
www.housespirits.com

Indio Spirits
Portland, OR
503-620-0313
www.indiospirits.com

Kolani Distillers
Paia, HI
808-579-8032
www.kolanidistillers.com

LOFT Liqueurs
Emeryville, CA
510-595-3330
www.loftliqueurs.com

Modern Spirits
Monrovia, CA
626-771-9469
www.modernspiritsvodka.com

New Deal Distillery
Portland, OR
503-234-2513
www.newdealdistillery.com

Osocalis Distillery
Soquel, CA
831-477-1718
www.osocalis.com

Ransom Spirits
Sheridan, OR
503-876-5022
www.ransomspirits.com

Rogue Spirits
Portland, OR
503-546-3418
www.rogue.com

Solomon Tournour Company
Ukiah, CA
707-485-5112
www.solomontournourdistillery.com

Square One Organic Spirits
Novato, CA
415-209-0109
www.squareonevodka.com

St. George Spirits/Hangar One Distillery
Alameda, CA
510-769-1601
www.stgeorgespirits.com

Stone Barn Brandyworks
Portland, OR
503-775-6747
www.stonebarnbrandyworks.com

Sub Rosa Spirits
Dundee, OR
503-476-2808
www.subrosaspirits.com

Superfly Distilling
Brookings, OR
503-520-8005
www.superflybooze.com

Valley Spirits
Modesto, CA
209-484-0311
www.drinkvalleyspirits.com

Source: American Distilling Institute

★ GLOSSARY ★

Agave syrup: A honeylike sweetener that comes from the agave plant. Also called agave nectar.

Aloe juice: The juice, which has been ingested for centuries, from the aloe plant, a species of succulent plant known for its medicinal properties.

Apple butter: A thicker form of applesauce that's made by slowly cooking puréed apples until the mixture thickens into a spreadable condiment.

Averna: An Italian amaro made from roots, herbs, and citrus rinds.

Belle de Brillet: A pear liqueur that is made by infusing Cognac with the essence of pears.

Campari: A bitter Italian aperitif made from a blend of herbs, fruits, and botanicals.

Carpano Antica: An Italian sweet vermouth.

Chambord: A French raspberry liqueur made from cognac, honey, raspberries, blackberries, vanilla, and citrus peel.

Chartreuse: A French liqueur made by Carthusian monks from a secret blend of herbs, available in either yellow or green.

Cointreau: A French triple sec made from sweet and bitter orange peels.

Crème de cassis: A black currant liqueur.

Cynar: An Italian bitter aperitif combining more than a dozen herbs and plants, most notably artichoke.

Demerara sugar: An unrefined and granulated light brown sugar.

Domaine de Canton: A French liqueur combining cognac with fresh Vietnamese baby ginger.

Fernet-Branca: An Italian amaro made from a blend of herbs and spices.

Grand Marnier: A French liqueur combining cognac with bitter orange essence.

Hard cider: Alcoholic cider made from fermented apple juice.

Honey syrup: A blend of honey and water commonly used to sweeten cocktails.

Ice, cracked: This is like the ice you find in freezers at grocery stores. To make it at home, place large cubes in a plastic bag and hit them with the back of a spoon.

Ice, crushed: Common in swizzles and juleps. To make crushed ice, place cubes in a clean towel and pound with a mallet or muddler. Some blenders also have a crushed-ice setting.

Lillet blanc: A French aperitif wine that combines wine with citrus liqueurs and is aged in oak casks.

Loquat: A small fruit that grows on an evergreen shrub throughout Texas and other regions with warm climates; it has a flavor akin to an apricot.

Nigori: An unfiltered saké with a rich, creamy, sweet character.

Nitrous oxide: The gas used in chargeable whipped cream and soda siphons.

Nocino: A bittersweet walnut liqueur common in Northern Italy.

Punt e Mes: An Italian sweet vermouth.

Ramazzotti: An Italian amaro made from a blend of herbs, roots, and orange peel.

Rich simple syrup: A syrup made from granulated sugar and water in a 2-to-1 ratio (2 parts sugar to 1 part water) and commonly used to sweeten cocktails.

Shrub: A vinegar-based syrup made with fruit and sugar that is used to flavor cocktails.

Simple syrup: A syrup made from equal parts of granulated sugar and water that is commonly used to sweeten cocktails.

Southern Comfort: A New Orleans spirit that blends whiskey with fruit and spices.

Sugarcane syrup: A thick syrup that comes from evaporating the juice extracted from sugarcane.

Tomatillo: A relative of the tomato with an earthy, lemony flavor that is popular in Mexican and Southwestern cooking.

Turbinado sugar: A pale brown form of sugar made by crystallizing sugarcane extract, resulting in characteristically large crystals. It's similar to Demerara sugar, but milder in color and flavor.

★ INDEX ★

A

B

★ LIQUID MEASUREMENTS ★

A.C.

Barspoon = 1 teaspoon

1 teaspoon = ⅙ ounce

1 tablespoon = ½ ounce

2 tablespoons (pony) = 1 ounce

3 tablespoons (jigger)= 1½ ounces

¼ cup = 2 ounces

⅓ cup = 3 ounces

½ cup = 4 ounces

⅔ cup = 5 ounces

¾ cup = 6 ounces

1 cup = 8 ounces

1 pint = 16 ounces

1 quart = 32 ounces

750 ml bottle = 25.4 ounces

1 liter bottle = 33.8 ounces

1 medium lemon = 3 tablespoons juice

1 medium lime = 2 tablespoons juice

1 medium orange = ⅓ cup juice

dash = 6 drops